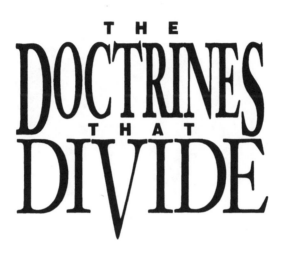

# THE DOCTRINES THAT DIVIDE

# Erwin Lutzer

# THE DOCTRINES THAT DIVIDE

## A Fresh Look at the Historic Doctrines That Separate Christians

kregel
PUBLICATIONS

Grand Rapids, MI 49501

*The Doctrines That Divide: A Fresh Look at the Historic Doctrines That Separate Christians*

Copyright © 1998 by Erwin Lutzer

Published by Kregel Publications, a division of Kregel, Inc., P.O. Box 2607, Grand Rapids, MI 49501.

Scripture quotations are from the New American Standard Bible, © the Lockman Foundation 1960, 1962, 1963, 1968, 1971, 1972, 1973, 1975, 1977.

ISBN 978-0-8254-3165-4

Printed in the United States of America

8 9 10 11 / 11 10 09

Dedicated to Elmer Towns
who taught me theology with enthusiasm,
who gave me wise counsel at a turning point in my life,
and who encouraged me as a writer.

# CONTENTS

# FOREWORD

Erwin W. Lutzer, pastor of the famed Moody Memorial Church in Chicago, has followed in the steps of his predecessors in the publication of this excellent book. He gracefully, artistically, and irenically deals with some of Christianity's major themes. He does so without hesitating to point out how error has crept into the Church of Jesus Christ. And it happens that many of the subjects he treats are central to contemporary theological discussions.

Christology today is at the center of major departures from historic orthodoxy. Lutzer discusses the deity of Christ and his human and divine natures. He faces the Mariology view of the Roman Catholic church and comes to grips with such questions as whether Peter was the first pope and the subject of justification by faith.

He plunges into early church history, the Reformation, and current discussions about free will, predestination, and the sovereignty of God that surround the Arminian-Calvinist viewpoints, and ends by asking whether a once-saved person can ever lose his salvation. All of this is enough to whet the appetite of any Christian and of those who stand on one side or the other of these issues or who know little or nothing about them. And those who do not agree with his conclusions will find solid arguments advanced that they must seriously consider.

Lutzer points out that evangelicalism is a divided house and that many of those in this camp are hopelessly inconsistent in that they entertain viewpoints that cannot be true when looked at logically and biblically. He gets into the sticky thicket of the "free will or omniscience" dilemma and does not hesitate to lock horns with scholars such as Clark Pinnock, who strongly endorses the notion of free will to the point where he limits the omniscience of God. The author denies that water baptism is essential to salvation. Yet, he is open-minded on the subject of the mode of baptism. When he tackles the subject of the Lord's Supper and the tough question about the presence of Christ in the elements, he ranges from that of the Catholic doctrine of transubstantiation, the Lutheran view of consubstantiation, the Calvinist view of a spiritual presence, and the Zwinglian view of a symbolic presence. The implications inherent in these positions are very important, and the reader can be assured that many will be unwilling to change their views, regardless of the arguments adduced. In all of this, there lies behind Lutzer's book the unstated but the perfectly apparent point that the most important function of the mind of those who call themselves Christian is to think Christianly. And there is a rarity of that among evangelicals. He is quite clear that we must be biblical, and to be biblical we must think Christianly.

Lutzer himself turns out to be a sturdy defender of the Reformation tradition, which has its antecedents not only in the Scriptures themselves but also in the struggles related to the views of Augustine and Pelagius who, broadly speaking, represent a common thread of opposing options that intrude themselves into virtually all of the points raised in this book. And that has to do with the nature of man subsequent to the fall of Adam and whether divine monergism, synergism, or man capable of lifting himself up by his own bootstraps is the biblical teaching. I recommend this book highly. The writer is a patient, persuasive pastor and never resorts to name-calling or condemnation of those who hold variant viewpoints. He does insist that some teachings are unbiblical, but he expresses loving concern for those who hold to what he considers to be unbiblical teachings. What more can we ask? Sell your bed and buy this book!

Harold Lindsell

# Why These Controversies?

This is a book about important doctrinal controversies
that exist within the broad spectrum of Christendom.
These are not trivial matters that can be set aside in the
interest of unity. Most of the issues discussed in this book
lie at the core of the gospel message. To understand why
and how these differences came about should be a high
priority for all thinking Christians.

In days gone by, many believers were tortured, eaten by
wild beasts, or burned at the stake because of their doctrinal convictions. Theology was appropriately called "the
Queen of the Sciences" because men believed that one's
relationship with God dwarfed all other considerations.
After all, what can compete with ultimate questions: Is
Christ qualified to be a Savior? Does baptism wash away
sins? Can we be sure of eternal life? How is God's grace
received by sinners? How many books are in the Bible?
Does God choose who will be saved? Once saved, can we
be lost?

Today opinion polls suggest that the Queen of the
Sciences needs a new dress; perhaps she has even lost her
crown. Only a small percentage of those who claim to be
born again know who preached the Sermon on the Mount

or can recite at least three of the Ten Commandments.
The wag who said that most Americans think that the
Epistles are the wives of the apostles was not very wide of
the mark! A friend of mine says that some of God's sheep cannot
tell the difference between grass and Astroturf! In the
midst of this doctrinal vacuum we hear pleas for unity. At
an ecumenical gathering, a prophecy purportedly came
from God the Father saying, "Mourn and weep for the
body of my Son is broken. Come before me for the body
of my Son is broken. . . . I gave all I had in the body and
blood of my Son. It spilled on the earth. The body of my
son is broken."

To dramatize an ecumenical spirit, the participants at
the conference had a foot washing service. Protestants
washed the feet of Catholic priests as a sign that they had
repented of teaching that Catholics were not Christians,
that the pope was the Antichrist, and that Catholic piety
was nothing but crude superstition. Catholics washed the
feet of Protestants, asking forgiveness for making jokes
about Martin Luther and other great Reformers and for
their smug disdain for Pentecostal worship.

Ecumenism is receiving much support in our day, even
from the public press. We've all read accounts telling us
that the Roman Catholic understanding of justification is
really much closer to Lutheranism than generally thought.
The optimists are predicting a merger of at least some
Protestant denominations with the church of Rome. To
quote George Cary in his book *A Tale of Two Churches*, "I
have high hopes not only for an increase in mutual understanding but also for the eventual reunion of the two
streams of Western Christendom." He believes that this is
necessary to fulfill the prayer of Christ, "that they may be
one."

During the early centuries of Christianity, the church
was perceived as unified, particularly as Rome became
the center of Christian leadership. As the papacy devel-

oped, with its network of bishops and priests, organizational unity was maintained. The first major split came in the year A.D. 1054 when the bishop of Rome asked that the bishop of Constantinople submit to his authority, but the request was refused. The division that had actually been developing for centuries now became a clean break and the Greek Orthodox church separated from Rome.

When the Reformation began in the sixteenth century, the Roman Catholic hierarchy predicted that once Christendom began to split, there would be no end to the fragmentation. A glance through a roster listing all of the denominations in the United States today demonstrates this prophecy was fulfilled. The number of different Baptist denominations alone proves the reality of organizational fragmentation.

Understandably, some would like to turn the clock back to pre-Reformation days, when the Western church was one monolithic organizational structure. The Catholic church has made many changes in the past twenty-five years; the rigidity of the past has given way to a new era of tolerance. Perhaps this is best exemplified in the Vatican II Council, which concluded that Protestants are no longer apostates but "separated brethren." If Protestants could just be a bit more flexible, and both sides were to give a little here and there, some think this vision of unity can be achieved. As this prophesy stated, the body of Christ is broken, and we have the responsibility of putting the pieces back together. It would be tragic indeed, the argument goes, if Christ's prayer for unity were left unfulfilled.

But to speak of unity and to minimize doctrinal differences is to sacrifice truth on the altar of wishful thinking. Unity, unless it is based on agreement regarding the content of the gospel, would not be worth the price. To this day, irreconcilable differences exist within Christendom on the most fundamental teaching of the gospel. As the chapters of this book will show, two divergent answers are still given to the question: What must I do to be saved? There is no need to repent for doctrinal differences if the truth of the gospel is at stake. When Peter began to misrepresent the gospel by withdrawing from the Gentiles and siding with the Jews who believed that circumcision was necessary for salvation, Paul rebuked Peter publicly: "But when I saw that they were not straightforward about the truth of the gospel, I said to Cephas [Peter] in the presence of all, 'If you being a Jew, live like the Gentiles and not like the Jews, how is it that you compel the Gentiles to live like Jews?'" (Gal.2:14).

Just giving the wrong *impression* about the content of the gospel gave Paul the right to rebuke publicly the most prominent apostle. There is no such thing as a harmless addition to the gospel. Indeed, Paul was so concerned about the purity of the message that he wrote, "If any man is preaching to you a gospel contrary to that which you received, let him be accursed" (Gal. 1:9). Without agreement on this central point, all attempts at unity are misguided.

Let me also say emphatically that the body of Christ is not broken. The unity for which Christ prayed has been granted by the Father. All true believers are members of Christ's body, which is indivisible. Paul did urge us to "preserve the unity of the Spirit in the bond of peace" (Eph. 4:3), but it was not organizational unity that he had in mind. The unity of the Spirit exists among believers despite their doctrinal differences. That we should maintain it, but not create it, was Paul's plea.

## Why Can't We Agree?

But why can't all of Christendom agree, at least on the essentials? After all, we have the same Bible and believe in the same Christ. Is this proof, as some suggest, that the Bible can be interpreted in so many different ways that it has no clear message? Many give up in despair, believing

that there is no way to arbitrate between conflicting
views. Even worse, they think there is no objective truth
at all. Your belief may be true for you; mine is true for me.
Why should we discuss it? The question is fair enough. Why can't we agree about
baptism, the Lord's Supper, the freedom of the will, or
even the most basic question, What must I do to be saved?
Is it really true that the Bible is like putty in a man's hand,
able to be molded into any shape one desires? Is it also
true that no one shape is better than another?
The fault is really not with the Bible. Its contents are,
for the most part, rather straightforward. Our disagreements are largely of our own making. That there should
be some disagreements is understandable. Imagine reading
the whole Bible for the first time, trying to grasp what it
teaches about Christ, God, man, angels, salvation, and
prophecy. No one book or section is a complete treatise
on a particular topic. Dealing as it does with such a vast
number of subjects, all of which touch ultimate issues, we
can understand why different interpretations would
occur. Yet to dismiss doctrinal controversies as hopeless
because "everyone has a right to his own private interpretation" is to ignore the fact that the basic message of the
Bible is remarkably clear. We, not the text, are the causes
of the problem. A number of reasons for the differences of
opinion can be given.
First, there are the *limitations* of men. For example,
several chapters in this book are devoted to the problem
of free will versus predestination. For reasons that will
become clear in those chapters, it is understandable that
people would line up on different sides of the issue. No
doubt part of our problem is that we do not have all the
pieces of the puzzle. God's relationship to the human will
involves some mystery. In some cases God may direct
man to act in one way, in another instance his involvement
may be minimal. No one can say he sees the whole picture. Differences are bound to exist.

Then we must admit that some passages are obscure.
Add to this the fact that we are limited in our understanding of the languages and culture of the Bible. The study of
Hebrew and Greek and even archaeology can illuminate a
particular passage whose meaning is otherwise unclear.
A fundamental principle is that no one verse should be
the basis for interpreting other clear passages. For example, if Acts 2:38 were the only verse in the Bible on the
doctrine of salvation, we might conclude that baptism is
necessary for salvation. Peter says, "Repent, and let each
one of you be baptized in the name of Jesus for the forgiveness of your sins; and you shall receive the gift of the Holy
Spirit." But if Peter means we must be baptized to be
saved, he would be contradicting dozens of other passages
in the New Testament where baptism is not a requirement
for salvation. This is a clue that Peter may have had other
reasons in mind for speaking of repentance and baptism in
the same breath. The chapter on baptism will discuss this
more fully.

Human limitations account for many differences of
opinion. But this factor should not be overdrawn. The
major doctrines of Scripture are clear enough to those
eager to learn. I've known new converts who knew
nothing of the Bible and yet have come to a reasonably
good understanding of doctrine by reading it on their
own without the benefit of teachers and commentaries.

Second, there is the *perversion* of man. Here we come
to those differences of opinion that come about because
of our bias; we make the Bible say what we want it to say
and for a variety of reasons.

For example, human nature, being what it is, resists the
notion that we can contribute nothing toward our salvation but must receive it freely by faith. It seems more
reasonable to say that we must earn eternal life and win
God's favor by our efforts. Predictably, such teachings
surface early in the history of the Church. Rituals arise
that are believed to make sinners worthy of eternal bless-
edness. As time progressed, the teaching of the New

Testament was lost in a maze of good works, sacraments, political intrigue, and even blackmail. Grace was no longer free but dispensed by the church in exchange for certain favors.

Prejudice dies hard. We've all met people who would never give up cherished doctrines *even if they became convinced that such teachings were unscriptural.* "I was raised a [choose one] Catholic, Anglican, Presbyterian, Baptist, Calvinist, or whatever, and I will die one!" The hidden assumption is "I'm not open to rethinking what I believe. Whether my beliefs are true or not is not of primary importance. I like what is familiar; I don't want to deny my upbringing. I'm comfortable, so leave me alone." The truth is, few people have an open mind, especially about matters of religion. Fewer still would actually change churches, even if they became convinced theirs was biblically off base. Thus, perverted doctrines and prejudices are easily perpetuated from one generation to another.

Third, there is the *unbelief* of man. Here I am thinking of those Bible interpreters who deny the miracles in Scripture because of the modern presupposition that miracles don't happen. Both Testaments are reinterpreted to fit the naturalistic mind-set. The German theologian Rudolf Bultmann found it necessary to "demythologize" the New Testament to make it palatable to twentieth-century theological appetites.

Such scholars tell us much more about themselves than the Bible. They have established their own criterion for truth and judge the Scriptures by it. In effect, such interpreters are writing their own autobiographies. Standing in judgment of the Bible, they put their own prejudices on display for all to see. The humanitarian Albert Schweitzer, when speaking about the many scholars who wrote their own life of Christ, said, "Each individual created Him in accordance with his own character. There is no historical task which so reveals a man's true self as the writing of the life of Jesus." Then Schweitzer went on to write his own life of Christ that pictured Jesus as mentally unstable! Theological liberalism has divided Christendom for centuries. Witness the rise of the Unitarians and other denominations that have denied the basic fundamentals of the faith. In varying degrees, liberalism has made inroads in denominations such as the Lutherans, Anglicans, Presbyterians, Methodists, and Baptists. These divisions are not simply the result of different interpretations. It is not the *interpretation* of the Bible as much as the *authority* of the Bible itself that is the issue.

Fourth, there is *tradition*. Rather than let the Bible stand as a complete revelation from God, the tendency of human nature is to fill in the gaps, to revere the teachings and additions of previous generations. The motive in accepting tradition is usually a noble one, namely, to clarify matters that the Bible itself does not address. For example, we all could wish that the Bible would give explicit teaching on infant salvation. We would like to be assured not only that infants are saved, but understand how they can be saved, since they are born under the condemnation of Adam's sin. On these matters the Bible is silent, giving us only vague hints as to what we should believe. However, consistent with man's desire to fill in the blanks, the teaching arose that when an infant is baptized the guilt of original sin was washed away. This tradition eventually became a dogma and was given the same authority as biblical doctrines.

Once the *principle* of tradition was admitted as a legitimate source of doctrine, the way was open for all kinds of other teachings to be accepted by the church. The exaltation of Mary, prayers to saints, the perpetuation of Peter's authority, and a host of other doctrines not explicitly found in the New Testament were considered as authoritative as the Bible itself.

Catholics and Protestants disagree over the value of tradition. The fundamental principle of the Reformation was *Sola Scriptura*, that is, the Scriptures alone are the rule of faith and practice. On the other hand, Catholicism gives tradition the same level of authority as the Bible. To quote the words of Pope John Paul, "Both Scripture and Tradition must be accepted and honored with equal feelings of devotion and reverence."

But tradition is seldom neutral. Almost always it detracts from the truth and distorts the clarity of the message. Jesus chided the Pharisees for nullifying the Word of God by their traditions.

In the chapters that follow, I will present a brief history of some major doctrines that have been a focal point for controversy. Again and again we will have to face the question of why the disagreements arose and why they continue to exist.

No concerned Christian can run and hide. The modern tendency to speak of the relevance of Christianity without bothering to examine its basic doctrines is misguided. Only when we stand on the foundation are we qualified to build the superstructure. This book is written with the hope that Christians will know what they believe and why.

Some will disagree with my conclusions, but all must agree that these issues are not trivial or irrelevant. Doctrine is an attempt to clarify what God has said about ultimate issues—Christ, heaven, hell, salvation.

The following chapters discuss some famous controversies that every mature Christian must resolve in his own mind. The old adage, attributed to Richard Baxter, "In necessary things, unity; in doubtful things, liberty; in all things, charity" is the spirit with which our search for truth must begin.

The chapters of this book need not be read in sequence. You might be interested in a particular topic—baptism, communion, or predestination versus free will. Regardless of where you begin, I pray that you will be challenged to think about some basic issues that must be settled in the minds of all growing Christians.

# Is Christ Truly God?

You might recall the ad that appeared in many newspapers back in 1982 proclaiming: "CHRIST IS NOW HERE." Our Lord Maitreya, the long-awaited world ruler, had arrived.

Buried in the fine print was the statement that this man was known by Christians as the Christ; Jews called him the Messiah; Buddhists called him the fifth Buddha; Muslims called him Imam Mahdi; and Hindus called him Krishna. Then came the punch line: *These are all names for the same person.*

I didn't expect to find this kind of heresy in the church. But one evening at a religious gathering I found myself seated next to a popular woman pastor who skillfully blends Christianity with the New Age movement, which teaches that God exists within every person and simply is awaiting discovery. "Do you believe that Christ is the only way to God?" I asked, quite sure that she would deny such an exclusive claim. "Of course I believe Christ is the only way to God," was the direct reply. "What makes you think I wouldn't believe that?"

But I persisted. "Do you believe that all the religions of the world are equally valid?" I asked, forcing her to define her doctrine with more precision. "Yes, I do," she answered candidly.

"Then how does this square with the view that Christ is the only way to God?" I asked, puzzled at what seemed to be a contradiction. *"When I speak about Christ, I am not speaking about Jesus of Nazareth"* was her honest reply. For her, the name *Christ* was generic, to be used for whatever god one wished. Christ was the one universal that exists in every person. This Christ, she candidly admitted, was not the Jesus of the Bible.

Theology has always been important, but never more so than today. Unwittingly, the church is imbibing old heresies without recognizing it. That's why we must return to the early councils of the church. They were convened to clarify doctrine, to pinpoint heresy, and to give a rationale for Christian beliefs. Given the popular widespread misconceptions of Christianity, it is time we returned to the basics. If we don't, thousands of people who believe they are Christians will discover in the day of judgment that they were misled.

The Council of Nicaea, which met in A.D. 325, defined the most important doctrine of Christendom. Out of that gathering two primary views about Christ emerged. Though they differed in wording by only a single letter of the Greek alphabet (an *iota* if you please), the bishops uncovered a theological chasm, which is with us until this day. On the one side are those who speak well of Christ but believe he is somewhat less than God; on the other are those who believe that Christ is God of very God. This council showed why it is possible to believe in Christ yet be damned forever. Thousands who call themselves believers will someday discover to their horror that they *believed in the wrong Christ.* More of that later.

Suppose you were reading the New Testament for the first time. How would you interpret Christ's prayers to God the Father? Would you conclude that he was less than God? And if he is God, was he only talking to himself?

The early church confronted a puzzling paradox. On the one hand, Christ was presented as being distinct from

God the Father. The Father spoke to Christ as his baptism; Christ, in turn, spoke to the Father often in prayer. Yet on the other hand, Christ was clearly presented as God; as Isaiah predicted, the Messiah would be "the Mighty God" (Isa. 9:6).

The early church fathers, for the most part, did not have a clear conception of the Trinity. They realized that the New Testament presents Christ as God but did not immediately face the question of how such a doctrine could be reconciled with the fact that there is only one God. If Christ is God, yet distinct from God the Father, are there not two Gods? And if the Holy Spirit also is God, are there not three?

## One God or Three Gods

Think through this bit of theological history. To avoid believing in three gods, a teaching called "Monarchianism" spread throughout the church in the third century. This teaching (pronounced Mo-nar-chi-an-ism, which means "one ruler"), held that the so-called three persons were actually modes in which the one person manifested himself. Both Christ and the Holy Spirit are God the Father, but in a different guise. Just as the same man may be a father, a son, and a brother, so the one person of God the Father played different roles.

This form of Monarchianism affirmed the true deity of Christ, but was forced to conclude that the Father himself became incarnate. Noetus, one of its leaders, wrote, "When the Father had not yet been born, he became the Son, he of himself and not another."

Although Monarchianism affirmed both the unity of God and the deity of Christ, it was judged as heresy. It could not satisfactorily account for those instances in which Christ spoke to his Father, for it would have to conclude that Christ was speaking to himself. Or in what sense could the Father forsake the Son on the cross if the

Son was simply the Father in a different role? Did the Father forsake himself?

Tertullian of North Africa (ca. 160–215), one of the first theologians to affirm the tri-personality of God, accused the Monarchians of denying the Holy Spirit and believing that God the Father was crucified. This doctrine was never a serious threat to Christendom as a whole. Though it still survives today among some who belong to the Jesus Only sect, it has largely passed off the scene.

Of course, we can fall into this ancient heresy when we thank God the Father for dying on the cross for us. Doctrinal accuracy requires that the persons of the Trinity be kept distinct.

But we are already ahead of the story.

## Setting the Stage

After the emperor Constantine was converted to Christianity in A.D. 312, he issued an edict that granted toleration to the Christian religion and in essence proclaimed Christianity the religion of the empire. He inherited a church that was seething with discussion regarding the person of Christ. To us moderns, theology is confined to the classroom, but in those days everyone was caught up in the debate. One bishop described Constantinople as preoccupied with these discussions. He said that if you asked someone for change in the marketplace, he would discuss with you whether Christ was begotten or unbegotten. If you asked about the quality of bread, you would receive the answer that "God the Father is greater, the Son is less." If you suggested that a bath was desirable, you would be told that "there was nothing before God the Son was created."[1]

Confused by these theological debates, Constantine was persuaded to convene a general council at Nicaea to resolve the bitter disputes. He hoped a consensus could be reached and reconciliation brought about. If not, the church could not unite the empire. In those days religious unity was the foundation for political unity.

## Outlining the Issues

Let's get some perspective on the views that were debated in various parts of the country.

Back in the previous century (about A.D. 250), Origen, a theologian from Alexandria in Egypt, asserted that the Son was subordinate to the Father. He sometimes even referred to the Son as the *Theos Deuteros*—the second God. Yet strangely, he also claimed to believe in the deity of Christ. Exactly what he meant by the subordination of the Son to the Father is unclear.

Arius, a presbyter in Alexandria, took Origen's view a step farther. If the Son has a different essence from the Father, it is logical to suppose that he is a created being. This would explain the subordination of the Son to the Father in such passages as John 14:28 where Christ said, "I go to the Father, for the Father is greater than I." Other relevant passages are Mark 13:32; John 5:19; and 1 Corinthians 15:28.

"If the Father begat the Son, he that was begotten had a beginning of existence," Arius said. "And from this it was evident, that there was a time when the Son was not."

Arius believed that the Son was created out of nothing, but he was the first and the greatest of the beings brought forth by God. Through the Son the world was created. The Son is worthy of worship because he was adopted by God.

This view was acceptable to those who were influenced by the paganism of the times. If you don't think that theology is often affected by the prevailing philosophy of the day, just think about how neatly the idea of a created Christ fit the mind-set of Greek thought.

The Gnostics (pronounced nos-tics, from the Greek word for *knowledge*) believed that matter was evil and, therefore, it was not possible for God to become man. If he were to do so, he would become tainted with evil. They claimed they had hidden knowledge, which led them to the conclusion that there was one supreme God who dwells alone, but there are many lesser gods who do

God's work, passing between heaven and earth. Christ could be considered as the greatest of these created gods and thus fit quite well within the context of Greek philosophy. To the pagan mind this was an acceptable theory, more believable than the doctrine that Christ, the Word, existed from all eternity and was equal to God the Father. As mentioned, if God became man, he would have been tainted with corruption. To make Christ less than God fit the pagan philosophy of the day.

Arius' views became influential because he was skilled in communication. He put his ideas into jingles, which soon became popular with the common people in the marketplace or children at school.

Today many cults find their champion in Arius. The Jehovah's Witnesses, for example, believe that Christ is *a* god but not fully God. To quote one of their founders, Charles Russell, "Being God's first creation, he was with the Father in heaven from the beginning of all creation, Jehovah God used him in the creating of all other things that have been created." Verses such as Colossians 1:15 and Revelation 3:14, where Christ is called "the beginning of the creation of God," are used to show that Christ was the first of the created beings.

Arius represented these views at the Council of Nicaea. He had gained a considerable following, and now the church had the opportunity to evaluate his position in the light of the Scriptures.

The opposite position was defended by the great theologian and apologist Athanasius (ca. 296–373). A champion of orthodoxy, he insisted that Jesus Christ was fully God and had the same essence as the Father. Specifically, he argued for the doctrine of the trinity, that God was a tri-unity. He affirmed that the following propositions could be held without contradiction: (1) Christ and the Holy Spirit are both fully God; (2) both are, in some sense, distinct from one another and from the Father; and (3) God is One.

Athanasius believed the three persons were not separate, which would lead to polytheism, but shared oneness of substance or essence. As church historian, Reinhold Seeberg wrote that Athanasius realized that "only if Christ is God without qualification, has God entered humanity, and only then have fellowship with God, the forgiveness of sins, the truth of God, and immortality been certainly brought to men."

It seems clear that either Christ was God or he was created. But every council has someone who believes he has found a compromise that will satisfy both parties. Historian Eusebius of Caesarea led a large middle party that claimed it could bridge the gap between the other two views. He sided with the Arians by saying that Christ was of a different substance from God the Father, but agreed with Athanasius that Christ was divine. He suggested that the nature of Christ be described as *homoiusios* (similar) to that of God the Father. Christ would be *like* God, but he would not *be* God without qualification.

So the stage was set for one of the most important church councils in history. Which of the three views would win the day?

## The Council Meets

Constantine realized that these differences were about to tear his Empire apart. He had chosen to move the capital of the empire from Rome to Byzantium (later the city would be named Constantinople in his honor; the modern name is Istanbul). So he asked the delegates to come to Nicaea, just 25 miles from the new capital. Thus in A.D. 325, 318 bishops met to wrestle with the question of the deity of Christ and the Trinity. Just think of the circumstances! Here were men who had been persecuted for their faith just a few years before. Many of them could show scars of their days of torture. Yet now, because of the

conversion of Constantine, they went openly to the
council, all expenses paid by the emperor!

Constantine himself gave the opening speech. He
reminded the bishops that they had to resolve these
theological matters because division in the empire was
worse than war. He hoped for a quick and amiable resolu-
tion.[2]

Arius was invited to state his views, that Christ was a
created being, that he was the first and the greatest of the
created beings, but created nonetheless. "The Son had a
beginning, but God is without beginning."

The assembly soon denounced this as heresy. Blasphemy. That much was settled.

More difficult, however, was the challenge of Eusebius
of Caesarea. He was both a personal friend of the emperor
and an admirer of Arius. So he presented his compromise.
Christ can be called God, but his substance is different
from that of God the Father.

But most of the bishops present believed that if Christ
had a different substance than the Father, he could not be
called God in the full sense of the term. Only if he had the
*same* substance could he be God.

The position of Athanasius was then presented. This,
you will recall, was the belief that Christ was "true God of
true God, begotten not made, of one substance with the
Father." The Greek word used was *homoousion*, "of one
substance." This creed could not be interpreted in any
other way than to say that Christ was God without qualification.

After several days of debate, the emperor saw that the
compromise of Eusebius would not be adopted. A consensus was developing toward the view that Christ was of the
*same* substance as God the Father. Thus the emperor
decided to intervene and side with Athanasius, who had
insisted that Christ was fully God, of one substance with
the Father. Thus the Nicene Creed emerged:

"I believe in one God the Father Almighty; Maker of

heaven and earth . . . And in one Lord Jesus Christ, the only begotten Son of God, begotten of the Father before all worlds. God of God, Light of Light, very God of very God, begotten, not made, being of one substance with the Father."

All but two of the bishops signed the creed. These two, along with Arius, were sent into exile. Constantine held a great banquet to celebrate the outcome, believing that his empire would now be unified. Eusebius, who had lost on the compromise position but later signed the new creed, wrote that all the bishops were present at the table of the emperor, with bodyguards and soldiers standing with sharp swords drawn . . . and among them the men of God could walk fearlessly. "Easily one could imagine this to be the kingdom of Christ or regard it as a dream rather than a reality."

But the victory was clouded. Some of the delegates believed that it was Constantine's influence that determined the outcome. After all, he had thrown his political weight behind Athanasius. Thus some dissenters argued that the outcome was based on political rather than theological considerations.

Athanasius himself was displeased that Constantine had personally entered the debate. He would rather have convinced the delegates by his own arguments than to have the dispute settled by a politician.

Unfortunately, the debate was far from settled. Arianism spread though many of the churches and subsequent emperors sided with whatever party had the majority at the time. Dissenters were banished. Athanasius continued to oppose Arianism with such tenacity that when told that everyone was opposing him he said, "Athanasius against the world!" Five times he was driven into exile, but he never wavered in his commitment to the full deity of Christ.

Later the Arians began to disagree among themselves and their influence waned. The council of Rome (341) and the council of Constantinople (381) ratified the Nicene Creed, which is the basis of orthodoxy to this day.

Is the Nicene Creed theologically correct? Sometimes it is said that the Bible nowhere says explicitly that Christ is truly God, sharing the divine essence with God the Father. But the following passages directly affirm the full deity of Christ (Isa. 9:6; John 1:1; Rom. 1:5; Heb. 1:8). In addition, there are dozens of other passages where Christ is *indirectly* declared to be God because the attributes of deity are ascribed to him.

What about those references that speak of Christ as "the beginning of the creation of God" (Col. 1:15; Rev. 3:14)? In both instances, the word used is *prototokos,* which means *first-bearer.* Christ is the preeminent One over all creation. Even if the word be translated *firstborn,* this would not imply that Christ was the first being to be created. Though Jacob was younger than his brother, Esau, Jacob was the firstborn. It is not a matter of time but status that determines who the *firstborn* is. Christ is the preeminent One.

## Why Is This Important to Me?

Critics have sometimes been amused that the Council of Nicaea split over one "iota." Remember that the difference between the words *similar* and *same* in Greek is but one letter of the alphabet, the letter "i." It is just like theologians to split hairs, arguing over minutae that have little to do with the real world. How much better to help the poor or get involved with the politics of the day!

William E. Hordern tells a story that illustrates how a single letter or comma can change the meaning of a message. Back in the days when messages were sent by telegraph there was a code for each punctuation mark. A woman, touring in Europe, cabled her husband to ask whether she could buy a beautiful bracelet for $75,000.

The husband relayed the message back "No, price too high." The cable operator, in transmitting the message, missed the signal for the comma. The woman received the message which read, "No price too high." She bought the bracelet; the husband sued the company and won! After that, the users of the Morse code spelled out punctuation. A comma or an "iota" can make a big difference when communicating a message![3]

Although Nicaea was divided over the Greek words *similar* and *same,* the issue was incredibly important. The theologians of past centuries understood that all other social and moral issues cannot compare with the significance of the doctrine of the deity of Christ. The real question is whether Christ is capable of being the Savior of mankind.

Even if Christ were the highest and most noble creature of God's creation, God would then only be indirectly involved in the salvation of fallen man. Salvation would have cost God little. One of his creatures would have suffered for mankind; God would have delegated "the dirty work."

But could salvation have been brought about if God had delegated the suffering to one of his creatures? No. Only God himself can reconcile man to himself. As Bishop Moule put it, "A Savior not quite God would be like a bridge broken at the farthest end." The consistent teaching of the Bible is that God suffered; that is why we can say *salvation is of the Lord.*

Think of it this way: God needed a ransom so that man might be forgiven, but only he could meet his own demands. A judge in California declared a man guilty of a misdemeanor and handed out a sentence. But he then left the bench and *paid the penalty he had demanded.* In salvation, God both declares us guilty and pays our debt. Only he can satisfy his own requirements. A savior less than God would be disqualified; God must do it himself.

The deity of Christ must also be affirmed to keep us from idolatry. Christ here on earth accepted the worship and prayers of people without a hint of embarrassment. He also forgave sin. The Jews of his day understood the implications with clarity and asked: "Who can forgive sins but God only?"

We have all wondered, "Is it OK to pray to Jesus?" It is true that Christ taught that we should pray to the Father in his name. But prayer to Christ is proper, too, for he is God without qualification. In heaven the Son is worshiped along with God the Father.

Several years ago, Bishop Pike, who denied all the major doctrines of Christianity, wrote a book entitled *The Other Side*. It is the story of how he tried to make contact with his son who had committed suicide. When Pike finally reaches his departed boy though a medium, father and son have a dialogue. So the father asks his son (in reality a demon impersonating his son) whether there is much talk about Christ on "the other side," to which the voice replies, "No, we don't talk about him much down here!"

Be assured of one fact: If after death you should find yourself in a place where there is not much talk about Jesus, you may be sure that you have ended up on the wrong side of eternity. The Book of Revelation is filled with hymns of praise and worship to Christ, the Lamb.

Christ tells us that he is the Alpha and the Omega, the Beginning and the End. The *Encyclopedia Britannica* comes in thirty heavy volumes, packed with information. Yet the writers never had to go outside of the twenty-six letters of the alphabet to write all that history, geography, and science. So it is with Christ. We need not go outside of him to find all the spiritual truth and wisdom we need. In him dwells all the fullness of the Godhead bodily.

If Christ is not God, then God has not saved us, and the worship that Christ accepted and his ability to forgive sins would have been blasphemous.

## Which Christ Saves?

Let us return to the conversation I had with that pastor about the person of Christ. She believed that Christ was the only way to God but also affirmed that all the religions of the world were an expression of the Christ. Remember, she said the Christ she proclaimed was not Jesus of Nazareth.

Now we are in a better position to understand why thousands of people who believe in Christ will be lost. *They have believed in a Christ who is not qualified to save them.* In effect, they have believed in an Antichrist of one form or another. "By this you know the Spirit of God: every spirit that confesses that Jesus Christ has come in the flesh is from God; and every spirit that does not confess Jesus is not from God; and this is the spirit of the antichrist, of which you have heard that it is coming, and now is already in the world" (1 John 4:2-3).

I have learned never to let a person tell me that he believes in Christ without asking, "Which Christ?" Albert Schweitzer, the humanitarian, believed in a Christ who was essentially insane; Rudolf Bultmann, the German theologian, believed in a mythological Christ; Immanuel Kant, the German philosopher, believed in a human Christ; many modern cultists believe in a created Christ.

The New Age movement that is gaining wide acceptance teaches that all the religions of the world are essentially the same, and their point of unity lies within the power of the mind. And according to some, this power should be called *Christ.* Even Mother Teresa, who is so highly praised by evangelicals, says that conversion means coming face to face with God as we accept him in our lives. "We become a better Hindu, a better Muslim, a better whatever we are. . . . What God is in your mind you must accept."[4] Apparently she believes that the Christ of Christianity is not necessary for conversion.

French priest Teilhard de Chardin expounded a new

theology in which the soul is the driving force of evolution. He taught that man was emerging into a new being ennobled by the universal spirit of the cosmic Christ. Christ is but a rung on the ladder of evolution.

But the most implicit faith, if placed in a Christ who is unable to save, will not get us to heaven. The question is, which Christ saves?

To answer that question we must return to the Nicene Creed. Only an incarnate Christ who is fully God qualifies to be a Savior.

## The Trinity

As already indicated, to affirm the deity of Christ is to believe in the Trinity. For if Christ is God, yet distinct from God the Father, there must be at least two persons in the Godhead. But since the Bible also affirms that the Holy Spirit is God, the Godhead must exist as a triunity.

In his book *The Trinity,* Augustine further developed Nicene theology. He stressed the unity of essence and the trinity of persons in the Godhead. But he was careful to point out that they are not like human persons who are separate entities; rather, they have mutual interpenetration and interdwelling.

Augustine admitted that the word *person* is not a good term to use because it implies polytheism, but he used it "not in order to express [the relationship], but in order not to be silent." He realized that no words can properly express the trinitarian relationship. *Person* conveys a sense of individuality and separateness; *mode* is too impersonal.

One professor said, "If we could strip *person* of its sense of individuality or *aspect* of its impersonal quality, either would serve."

An analogy might help. Augustine said that because man was created in the image of God, his mind was an example of the Trinity: Memory, intelligence, and will each share the same substance, yet they are distinct in function. Yet

Augustine's illustration fails because these functions are too impersonal. We must affirm three persons, but sharing one substance.

Sometimes the charge is made that Christians believe a contradiction—that one equals three. This, of course, is false. We are not saying that one God equals three Gods, but that one God is revealed in three "persons," understanding that the word *person* cannot be interpreted in an individualistic sense.

## Upon This Rock

The deity of Christ, then, is the foundation of Christian doctrine. It is not enough to believe in Christ, but to believe in a Christ who is able to save. *The amount of faith is not as important as the object of faith.* You may believe that the ice on a pond is strong enough to hold your weight, but if it is but a half inch, you will still fall through. Conversely, you may have doubts as you walk on ice a foot thick, but it will hold you despite your fears.

Faith alone does not save; only faith in a person qualified to save brings salvation to the human heart. Not all who say "Lord, Lord," will enter into the kingdom of heaven. The Christ of the cults is unable to pay the penalty for sin. To believe in a Christ who is less than God is to have faith that is misplaced.

The Council of Nicaea divided Christendom forever. On the one side are those who speak well of Christ but affirm he is less than God; on the other are those who believe he is "God of very God." These two streams of thought flow in different directions never to meet.

We should be grateful that those who have preceded us in the history of the church insisted that we believe in the Christ who is God. In his own person he unites God and man; in his death he reconciles man to God. Salvation or damnation; heaven or hell. That is what Nicaea was all about.

## Notes

1. Bruce L. Shelley, *Church History in Plain Language* (Waco: Word Books, 1982), 113.
2. Shelley, 115.
3. William E. Hordern, *A Layman's Guide to Protestant Theology* (New York: Macmillan, 1955), 15-16.
4. Desmond Doig, *Mother Teresa: Her People and Her Work* (New York: Harper and Row, 1976), 156.

# TWO

# Is Christ Truly Man?

Back in the sixties, when "the death of God" theology was popular, a friend of mine was visiting door to door in a neighborhood in Dallas, witnessing for Christ. After a brief introduction the conversation went like this:

"Do you believe Jesus Christ was God?" the prospective convert asked.

"Yes, I sure do."

"Do you also believe that Jesus Christ died on the cross?"

"Yes, of course."

"Then get out of here!" the angry homeowner shouted. "I don't want to have anything to do with this theory that God died way back when!"

How would you have answered? Sounds logical, doesn't it? If Christ is God, and he died, then *God has died!* The easy answer is to say that his humanity died but his deity didn't. But if that is so, then a *man* died for our sins, and God was only indirectly involved at the cross. The conclusion would be that humanity, and not deity, paid the price of redemption.

No mystery has taxed the minds of theologians like that of the Incarnation. At Christmas many years ago, one of my daughters, then six years old, asked, "Who was looking after the world when God was a baby?" A good question, but difficult to answer.

Such questions vexed the minds of theologians during the fifth century when theological discussions permeated Europe. Various theories were advanced as to how the Incarnation was to be understood. Some stressed the humanity of Christ, others his deity. Some thought his two natures were mixed; others thought they were separate. If Christ were either fully man or fully God, we could more easily understand him. But because he is both, there always is a tendency to emphasize one nature at the expense of the other.

Remember Christ came into a culture that believed matter was inherently evil. To reinterpret Christianity to fit the prevailing ideas of the time, two approaches were taken. One was to deny the deity of Christ (we considered this in the last chapter), the other was to deny his humanity. Actually, the Gnostics did both.

## The Influence of Plato

We have all heard that philosophers are people who sit in ivory towers, seeking answers to questions that people never ask. This is a false stereotype. It is true that philosophers are speculative in their ideas, but the other side of the story is that they influence the controlling ideas of whole continents.

The famous Greek philosopher Plato (428–348 B.C.) was both a blessing and a curse to Christianity—a blessing because his philosophy conditioned the populace to think about abstract ideas and ultimate questions. To some, his teaching appeared to be compatible with Christianity because he believed in the immortality of the soul. But ultimately he was a curse to Christianity because his philosophy opposed the doctrine of the Incarnation. This challenge was as damaging as the physical persecution the believers received at the hands of the Roman Empire. The ideas of one brilliant man threatened the existence of the Christian faith.

Plato, you will recall, made a sharp distinction between the material world and the concepts of the mind (he called them *forms*). Matter was constantly subject to change and decay; ideas, on the other hand, had permanence and perfection. For example, I might judge that it is cold outside; you may think it is warm. Our bodies are subject to the relativity of our feelings and surroundings. But the idea that $2 + 2 = 4$ is constant. It is true even if you have a fever and the moon changes to green cheese!

And what does that have to do with the heresy that threatened the church? By saying that matter was inferior (evil), a future generation of Platonists concluded that it was not possible for God to assume the nature of manhood. As we already learned in the previous chapter, *for God to become man would mean that God had become imperfect.*

*Gnosticism,* as we noted, was a powerful movement that challenged Christianity in the second and third centuries. Like Plato, the Gnostics were convinced that God could have no contact whatever with matter because it is evil. And yet they insisted that they could combine their theories with Christianity. To do so, they had to explain how God could have created the world with all of its evil and yet be blameless. That he could have actually become man was unthinkable.

There were two parts to their solution. First, God created (or emanated) a god who in turn created another who created another. . . . On and on it went for at least thirty times! This, they said, could explain how God could have created the world without getting too close to matter—which, remember, is inherently evil! Christ was really one of these created gods, sent to free us from the evil chains of matter into which we are locked. Thus, they denied Christ's deity.

Others said that Christ really didn't become man at all but only *appeared* to have a body. Even if he were one of God's created subordinates, if he became man, he still would have been contaminated. Though he was born of a virgin, he could not have escaped the corruption of the flesh. To preserve him from every taint of evil, this form of Gnosticism denied that Christ had a physical body. He only *seemed* to have such. They denied *both* Christ's deity and humanity.

These theories were already floating around during the first century. That is why John in his epistles wrote, "What was from the beginning, what we have heard, what we have seen with our eyes, what we beheld and our hands have handled, concerning the Word of life . . ." ( 1 John 1:1 ). John is saying that the disciples actually touched Christ. He wasn't a hallucination. In fact, the real test of doctrine is whether one believes that Christ is come in the flesh.

Though we as moderns debate the deity of Christ, the Christian church in those days had to defend his humanity with equal vigor. If matter is inherently evil, God could not possibly have contact with the world as Christianity teaches.

When John wrote, "The Word became flesh," the statement was explosive in its implications. For one thing it meant that the Platonic notion that flesh is intrinsically evil was false. For another it meant that God had taken a radical step by becoming closely identified with man and his needs. So the church was forced to affirm not only the deity of Christ, as it had done in the Council of Nicaea, but to affirm his humanity with equal clarity.

This explains why the Apostles' Creed, which arose during this time ( ca. 350), was so insistent on both the deity and humanity of Christ. First it affirmed that "God was the maker of heaven and earth." Then it specified that he "was born of the Virgin Mary and suffered under

Pilate," etc. The creed is, above all, an explicit affirmation of the humanity of Christ. Undoubtedly, it was intended to counter the prevailing Greek influence.

For more than a century (A.D. 350–450), debates raged regarding the person of Christ. Fortunately there were at least a few brilliant men who saw that Christianity could never be merged with the philosophies of this world without diluting its message. The city of Alexandria in Egypt was particularly influenced by the Greek philosophers, hence many of the Gnostics originated there. But Tertullian (ca. 160–215), also of North Africa, stood against this Greek influence and thundered, "What indeed has Athens to do with Jerusalem? What concord is there between heretics and Christians?" He stood firmly for the complete deity and humanity of Christ in the face of Gnostic influence.

Finally in A.D. 451, Pope Leo the Great asked the emperor Marcian to call a general council of the church to resolve the matter lest a variety of heresies go unchecked. The delegates met in Chalcedon to hammer out the wording of a creed that defined as far as possible the relationship between the divine and human natures of Christ. It was the fourth general council of the Christian church.

### Time Out for a Quiz

Imagine that you are one of the nearly four hundred delegates invited to attend the council of Chalcedon, a city just outside of Constantinople. One hundred and twenty-six years earlier, in 325, the council of Nicaea had affirmed that Christ was God, of the same substance as God the Father.

Now your agenda is to take the theological discussion a step farther and try to define the relationship between his deity and humanity. You are asked to vote on which of the following statements best describes the relationship between the divine and the human natures of Christ. Go ahead and vote—are these statements true or false?

1. Christ had a human body, but the spiritual (or rational) aspects of his nature were divine. Physically he was man, but rationally, spiritually, he was God. In other words, he did not have a human soul and spirit; all the immaterial aspects of his nature were divine.

2. In Christ, a man and God were joined together without intermingling, so that Christ is really two distinct persons. The human person gave himself to the divine person so that there was moral unity between them, but there is no *substantial* unity between them.

3. The human and the divine natures were fused in such a way that humanity participates in divinity. More accurately, Christ had only one nature. This nature was neither God nor human but a mixture of both. Like a drop of honey in a cup of water the two natures were mingled to produce a new third substance.

4. None of the above.

Now let us consider these views separately. The first was asserted by Apollinarius. He believed that if Christ had been fully human in body, soul, and spirit, he would have been sinful. Furthermore, human nature itself cannot be the object of adoration; therefore, to worship a Christ who was fully human would be idolatry.

The church correctly argued, however, that if Christ did not assume a full human nature, he could not be a sufficient representative of humanity and thus could not be our Redeemer. Manhood involves the spiritual dimensions of human nature as well as the physical. Christ must have possessed a human soul and spirit as well as a human body.

By the time the delegates met at Chalcedon in 451, Apollinarianism had already been rejected at a previous council in Constantinople in 381.

Many Christians today have Apollinarian tendencies without realizing it. Even the familiar line of a Christmas carol, "veiled in flesh the Godhead see," if not correctly interpreted, could be understood as Apollinarian. I've met many believers who assume that the physical body of Christ came from Mary, but all the immaterial aspects of his nature (soul and spirit) were divine. But he had to be fully human—body, soul, and spirit—to be our Redeemer.

The second view, that Christ was two persons, was popularized by the monk Nestorius. He became bishop of Constantinople in 428, a time when devotion to the Virgin Mary was growing. He denounced the idea that Mary was *theotokos,* the "God-bearer."

Nestorius feared that people might suppose that Mary, if called the "Mother of God," was the mother of Christ's divine nature. So he asserted that Christ was two persons, and Mary was the mother of only the human person who was united with the divine person. Thus, Christ was two people—the Son of man and the Son of God.

Nestorianism appeared to solve the problem of how Jesus Christ could suffer as man and yet be incapable of suffering as God. Quite simply, the Son of man suffered but the Son of God did not. Though there was union between the two persons, they remained essentially separate.

Nestorius is to be commended for his belief that Christ was truly man and truly God. But by believing that he was two distinct persons, he introduced a kind of schizophrenia into the church's understanding of Christ. Scholars were tempted to divide his sayings: those he spoke as man ("I thirst") and those he spoke as God ("Before Abraham was, I am").

But even more important, this view denies the Incarnation because there is no sense in which "the Word became flesh." At best the Word would have been *united* alongside of flesh.

Finally, this understanding makes the worship of Christ

difficult. To fall in worship before the Christ who walked this earth would be a form of idolatry, for the visible Christ is but a human person. People who saw Christ saw only a man, not God. For Nestorius, it was only the invisible divine person who could be properly worshiped.

At the Council of Ephesus in 431, Nestorius was condemned and given ten days to recant.

We can easily fall into the error of Nestorianism when we say that Christ was both God and man, if by that we mean he was God and also a man. The implication is that he was two separate persons. It is better to speak of him as the God-man to preserve the unity of his person.

The third view was held by Cyril, bishop of Alexandria, who gained fame in his condemnation of Nestorianism. He taught that the two natures of Christ were fused. Though there is some question as to whether or not he has been misinterpreted throughout the centuries, his view did eventually lead to monophysitism (pronounced mo-noph-y-sit-ism, meaning "one nature"). Christ had but one nature, since deity and humanity were blended together. Cyril felt this was necessary to protect the unity of Christ's person.

If Nestorius separated the God-man to the point where the only contact between the two natures was moral agreement, Cyril united them in such a way that the resultant natures was neither God nor man, but a mixture of the two. Eutyches, a controversial follower of Cyril, took this view to its logical conclusion and affirmed that Christ's body was essentially different from other human bodies. Through the union of the two natures, a third substance had been formed.

Other options were probably discussed at the Council of Chalcedon, but the three above were rejected. In their place, the council wrote a creed that was specifically aimed at combating these heresies.

Leo the Great dominated the debate at the council. He is known as a pope who advanced the primacy of the

Roman church, and made repeated reference to Christ's words in Matthew 16:19, "You are Peter, and upon this rock I will build My church," to substantiate the papacy. He was a great administrator and an effective preacher. He fought vigorously for the full humanity of Christ at a time when the Gnostics had stressed Christ's deity at the expense of his humanity. In A.D. 449 he had written a letter to Flavian, the bishop of Constantinople, that defended the traditional doctrine of the Incarnation. This document, known in history as Leo's *tome,* was the chief theological source used by the council.

## The Creed

The final statement was largely a denial of the views listed above. But some general statements are also made about the union of the two natures:

*We then following the Holy Fathers, all with one consent, teach men to confess one and the same Son, our Lord Jesus Christ, the same perfect in Godhead and also perfect in manhood; truly God and also truly man, of a reasonable soul and body; consubstantial with the Father according to the Godhead and consubstantial with us according to the manhood; in all things like unto us, without sin; begotten before all the ages of the Father according to the Godhead, and in these latter days, for us for our salvation, born of the Virgin Mary, the mother of God, according to the manhood; one and the same Christ, Son, Lord, Only-begotten, to be acknowledged in two natures, inconfusedly, unchangeable, indivisibly, inseparably, the distinction of natures being by no means taken away by the union, but rather the property of each nature being preserved, and concurring in one person and one subsistence, not parted or divided into two persons, but one and the same Son, Only-begotten, God the Word, the Lord Jesus Christ.*

Notice that the creed affirmed that Christ was fully man
(opposing Apollinarianism) but he was one person (opposing Nestorianism) with two natures that remained
distinct (opposing Monophysitism). By stating that the
attributes of both natures can be affirmed of one person,
the creed tried to help us catch a glimpse of what John
meant when he said, "The Word became flesh."

No attempt was made to explain precisely how the two
natures were united in the one person, for the delegates
knew they were on the precipice of mystery.

The creed also agreed that Mary was the mother of
God, not because she originated the divine nature, but
because she bore a child who was, in fact, divine. This
phrase was used not so much to exalt Mary as to accen-
tuate Christ's deity.


## The Implications

What does this have to do with us? Does it really matter
whether Christ was fully human?

If Christ were not fully human, he would have been
disqualified as the Savior of mankind. "Since then the
children share in flesh and blood, He Himself likewise
also partook of the same, that through death He might
render powerless him who had the power of death, that is,
the devil" (Heb. 2:14). In the last chapter we quoted
Bishop Moule as saying that a Savior not quite God would
be like a bridge broken at the farther end. But, of course, a
Savior not quite man would be like a bridge broken at *this*
end. Christ had to be fully man as well as God to redeem
us to himself. To redeem us—body, soul, and spirit—he
had to become one of us—body, soul, and spirit. Yes, he
was fully man.

Yet the council affirmed that Christ was united in one
person. To illustrate what this meant in Christ's earthly life
consider his temptation in the desert for forty days. Could
he have sinned? Nestorius who said that Christ was two

separate persons would probably have said, "Yes. Christ the Son of man could have sinned, but not Christ the Son of God."

But to say that Christ the man could have sinned but not Christ who is God, is to separate the two persons as Nestorius had done. The Bible doesn't say whether Christ could have sinned but merely that he didn't. But the decision of Chalcedon would logically, and I believe correctly, lead to the conclusion that Christ could not have sinned. *It would have been impossible for his humanity to sin without his deity being involved.* Thus the unity of his person makes Christ unable to sin.

As might be expected, some theologians have contended that if Christ were not capable of sinning, his temptation was but a charade. If he could not sin, then not only was Satan wasting his time, but Christ was really unable to appreciate our temptations because his were not real.

The reply is that the temptation was real in the sense that Christ felt the full force of the lust of the flesh, the lust of the eyes, and the pride of life. The purpose of the temptation from God's standpoint was not to see whether Christ would sin, but to prove that he wouldn't. Satan had to know that Christ was stronger than he; Christ had to feel what we are up against so that he could be a faithful and merciful High Priest. And we had to have an example of how we should deal with temptations when they come our way.

## Did God Die?

What about the person who says that if Christ is God we must logically conclude that God died? The answer is a qualified yes—deity did die. Christ could not have died without deity being involved. Of course, we should not think of death as annihilation; in that sense God is incapable of death. But if we think of death as separation—physical death is separation of the soul and body and spiritual death is separation from God—in that sense God the Son died. The fellowship of the Trinity was at least temporarily affected when Christ became sin for us. The total person, the God-man, paid the penalty for our sins.

That is why the Bible can teach that salvation is of the Lord. God the Son was suffering, paying the penalty for sin to God the Father. When Christ cried out on the cross, "My God, My God, why hast Thou forsaken Me?" he was speaking not just as man but as God. The God-man was bearing the sin of the world. Only the unity of the person could pay the price of redemption.

And finally, when will the union of the two natures in one person end? Never! The two natures, united in the womb of Mary, will never become separated. Christ had to become a man to be both a Savior and Priest. "But He, on the other hand, because He abides forever, holds His priesthood permanently" (Heb. 7:24). We shall see him in his glorified body, and the nail prints in his hands will still be visible. As King and High Priest he will be the God-man forever.

The councils of Nicaea and Chalcedon debated the cornerstone of Christianity, namely the person of Christ. These creeds defined the person of Christ for subsequent generations. Roman Catholics and Protestants agree that Christ was both man and God without qualification.

But now we turn our attention in the next chapters to other controversies that have never been finally settled. Yet their importance has never diminished.

# THREE

# Was Mary the Mother of God?

Stop for a moment and think of what it must have been like to be Mary, the young virgin chosen by God to give birth to the Son of God. Tradition says that every Jewish maiden hoped that she would be the one to have the honor of bearing the promised Messiah. And now, by means of an angel, the Lord tells Mary that she will conceive and bear a son who will fulfill all the Old Testament promises.

The excitement was mingled with sorrow. Mary would be misunderstood; some of her friends would not believe that she had conceived without sexual relations. Even Joseph thought she had been unfaithful until he had a dream that set the record straight.

Mary was, above all, a woman of a broken heart. She would not only be misunderstood but eventually would watch her son die a cruel death. As Simeon predicted, "A sword will pierce even your own soul" (Luke 2:35). For the privilege of bearing the Son of God there was a price to pay.

Understandably, the Christian church has always been fascinated with Mary; after all, she did give birth to a baby who is called God. What part did she have in this miracle?

And what honor is appropriate for this remarkable woman?

The New Testament itself says little about her. The angel Gabriel said to her, "Hail, favored one! The Lord is with you" (Luke 1:28). Elizabeth exclaimed, "Blessed among women are you, and blessed is the fruit of your womb!" (Luke 1:42). In the beautiful song we call the Magnificat, she acknowledges that future generations would call her *blessed,* but she said nothing about future generations bowing before her in adoration. The Gospel of Matthew explicitly states that she had other children by Joseph after Jesus was born. The names of his brothers were James and Joseph and Simon and Judas (Matt. 13:55).

But by the end of the second century a legend surfaced that *she* had had a miraculous birth. The idea also arose that she was a virgin all of her life. Tertullian, the famous theologian of North Africa, spoke against these legends and showed from Scripture that Mary and Joseph had a normal marriage relationship. We read that Joseph kept her a virgin *until* she gave birth to Christ (Matt. 1:25). Thereafter she had normal sexual relations.

But with the coming of Constantine, pagan ideas were absorbed into the church. As long as Christianity was a persecuted sect it largely retained its purity, but when it became the official religion of the Roman Empire, it incorporated Roman methods and ideas. Many people who came into the church brought with them superstitions and devotions to pagan gods that were transferred to Mary. As Boettner says, "Statues were dedicated to her, as there had been statues dedicated to Isis, Diana, and others, and before them the people kneeled and prayed as they had been accustomed to do before the statues of the heathen goddesses."[1]

Ancient Babylon had a mother-child cult that had been accepted by Rome and this in turn became incorporated into the church. Titles of honor were borrowed wholesale from these pagan gods, thus Mary was called "the Queen of Heaven," a title the pagans gave to the mother-child cult of Babylon. The Old Testament prophet Jeremiah refers to this abomination, scolding the people for paying tribute to the Babylonian practice of honoring "the queen of heaven" (Jer. 7:18; 44:17-19, 25).

The blending of paganism with Christianity can be seen in the development of the doctrine of "patron saints." Ancient religions had a god for practically every phenomenon—a god of the sea, war, hunting, good luck, and others. Saints were now given these special areas of responsibility. Thus, the faithful prayed to the designated saint when faced with a special need.

By the fifth century a debate raged as to whether or not Mary could appropriately be called "the Mother of God." As seen in a previous chapter, Nestorius was so concerned about the growth of the cult of Mary that he insisted that Christ was actually two separate persons—one divine, the other human. He thought that the myth of Mary could be countered by insisting that she gave birth only to the human person of Christ. But Nestorianism was condemned because it separated the person of Christ and actually denied the Incarnation. If Christ was two separate persons, then the Word did not actually become flesh.

As mentioned, the Creed of Chalcedon included the words, "Mary the Mother of God." But how should these words be understood? Obviously she did not originate the divine nature. But we can say that she participated in the origination of the human nature of a child who was divine. So it would be more accurate to speak of her as the mother of the God-man, recognizing that deity was miraculously joined with humanity in her womb. When the Council of Chalcedon used the phrase "the Mother of God," it did so not to honor Mary as much as to emphasize the deity of Christ.

Whether she was "the Mother of God" depends on how

the phrase is interpreted. There is nothing wrong with it as long as it is properly understood.

But there is more to the story.

## The Honors Granted Mary

Once Mary was accorded a place of special honor, various traditions about her were accepted. The following is a list of doctrines taken from a textbook entitled *Fundamentals of Catholic Dogma* by Ludwig Ott. Since it is used to instruct Catholic priests, it provides a helpful analysis of the place of honor she received.

Ott's textbook was published in 1952. We all know that changes have come about since the second Vatican Council of 1962. After we have studied what Ott has to say, we can turn to Vatican II to see whether Catholicism has modified its teachings about the Virgin.

One cannot understand Catholicism without understanding the role of Mary. She is not merely a woman who is highly exalted in Catholic teaching but is a symbol of Rome's understanding of salvation, as we will see later. If you are already acquainted with Roman Catholic theology, the following summary of the doctrines concerning Mary will provide a review.

*1. The Immaculate Conception* is the belief that Mary herself was conceived without original sin. A special soul was created by God and infused into the bodily matter prepared by her parents. Thus she was spared from the defect of original sin by the unmerited grace of God.

Though born without original sin, Mary still had to be redeemed. To quote Ott, "Thus Mary was redeemed 'by the grace of Christ' but in a more perfect manner than other human beings. While these are freed from original sin present in their souls ... Mary the Mother of the Redeemer was preserved from the contagion of original sin."[2]

Ott admits that this is not explicitly revealed in Scrip-

ture but says it is implicit in the words of the angel to
Mary, "Hail Mary full of grace!" (Luke 1:2, KJV). The grace
received by Mary must be of unique perfection. When
Elizabeth said to Mary that she was blessed among women,
the inference, according to Ott, is that the blessing of God
that rests upon Mary is parallel to the blessing given to
Christ in his humanity. This suggests that Mary, like Christ,
was free from sin.

Ott cites a number of the church fathers who agree
with this doctrine and says that since the seventh century
a feast was celebrated in the Eastern church that com-
memorates the Immaculate Conception. This feast was
later accepted by the Western churches. However, because
of the influence of Bernard of Clairvaux, who called the
doctrine an unfounded innovation, the leading theologians
of the twelfth and thirteenth centuries (including Thomas
Aquinas) rejected the Immaculate Conception. According
to Ott, they could not understand how Mary could be
born without sin and yet be in need of redemption.

The famous philosopher John Duns Scotus (1308)
argued that it is possible to reconcile Mary's freedom
from original sin with the fact that she also needed
redemption. We need not concern ourselves with the
technicalities of his argument except to say that the
controversy precipitated a heated debate between the
Dominicans (who followed Aquinas) and the Franciscans
(who followed Scotus). The Jesuits also sided with Scotus
and promoted the doctrine that Mary was sinless.

At any rate, the Council of Trent, which convened in
response to the Reformation of the sixteenth century,
affirmed the Immaculate Conception, but not until December 8, 1854, was the matter finally resolved. Pope
Pius IX, in a Papal Bull, said that the following doctrine
was revealed by God, and therefore to be believed by the
faithful, "The Most Holy Virgin Mary was, in the first
moment of her conception, by a unique gift of grace and
privilege of Almighty God, in view of the merits of Jesus

Christ, the Redeemer of mankind, preserved free from all stain of original sin."[3]

2. *Mary was free from personal sin.* The question the church then faced was whether or not Mary, who was born without original sin, ever sinned personally during her lifetime. Catholic Dogma affirms that although she was subject to general human defects just as Christ was, she nevertheless lived sinlessly. In particular, she did not have any inordinate sexual desires. By her love for God, faith, humility, and obedience, she acquired special merits that can be of benefit to the saints. The Council of Trent declared, "No justified person can for his whole life avoid all sins, even venial sins, except on the ground of a special privilege from God such as the church holds was given to the blessed Virgin."[4]

3. *She was perpetually a virgin.* That Mary was a virgin when she conceived Christ is, of course, taught in Scripture (Matt. 1:22). But the Catholic church went beyond this, and taught that she was a virgin to her death. She bore Christ without any violation of her physical virginity. Although she later married Joseph, the church believes that he and Mary did not have sexual relations. What is the Scriptural basis for this? Ott again agrees that this is not taught in the Bible, but may be inferred from the question that Mary puts to the angel, "How can this be, since I am a virgin?" (Luke 1:34). From this it is deduced that Mary took a vow of constant virginity.

4. *The bodily assumption of Mary into heaven.* Given the high exaltation of Mary in the traditions of Catholicism, we should not be surprised that the church believes that she, like Christ, ascended bodily into heaven. Thus, on November 1, 1950, Pope Pius XII promulgated the doctrine he said was revealed by God that "Mary, the immaculate perpetually Virgin Mother of God, after the completion of her earthly life, was assumed body and soul into the glory of heaven."[5]

But the veneration does not end, for Pope Pius also

taught that Mary "resplendent in glory in body and soul
reigns in heaven with her son."

Ott, in his attempt to defend this doctrine, modestly
again admits, "Direct and express scriptural proofs are not
to be had." But he argues that this doctrine logically
follows the other ones already listed—namely that she
was free from sin, a perpetual virgin, the mother of God
and that *she shared in the redemptive work of her son.*

## The Work of Mary

Although Christ is the sole mediator between God and
man, the Catholic church teaches that Mary has a secondary role in reconciling man and God. The Fathers called
Mary the Mediatrix, the "go-between" between God and
man. In fact, no grace is conferred on man without her
intercessory cooperation.

What is more, she is called the co-redemptrix, a word
coined in the fifteenth century to teach that she cooper-
ated in the act of redemption, suffering with Christ under
the cross. And according to Pope Pius XII, she was the
one who offered Christ on Golgotha to the Eternal Father.
Yet Mary is not to be thought of as a priest, but as sharing
in the suffering of Christ for sin.

To quote Ott:

*In the power of the grace of Redemption merited by
Christ, Mary, by her spiritual entering into the sacrifice
of her Divine Son for men, made atonement for the sins
of men and . . . merited the application of the redemptive
grace of Christ. In this manner she cooperates in the
subjective redemption of mankind.*[6]

So Mary cooperates in the application of the grace of
redemption to mankind. Though her intercession is by far
inferior to the prayers of Christ, it is nevertheless far
superior to the intercession of all other saints. Pope Leo

the XIII decreed that "nothing according to the will of God, comes to us except through Mary, so that, as nobody can approach the Supreme Father except through the Son, similarly nobody can approach Christ except through the Mother."[7]

## Comparison of Mary and Christ

In his book, *The Glories of Mary,* Cardinal Alphonse de Litouri, a devotional writer of the Catholic church, gives Mary a place of honor that competes with Christ for the devotion of men. The editor of the book says that it is a summary of Catholic tradition and is not merely the opinion of an individual but of the church itself. The author teaches that Mary cannot be praised too highly, for "whatever we say in praise to the Mother is equally praise to the Son."[8] Note the parallels to Christ in the following quotations:

"She is truly a mediatress of peace between sinners and God. Sinners receive pardon . . . by Mary alone."[9]

"The holy church commands a worship peculiar to Mary."[10]

"Mary is called . . . the gate of heaven because no none can enter that blessed kingdom without passing through her."[11]

"Our salvation is in the hands of Mary. . . . He who is protected by Mary will be saved, he who is not will be lost."[12]

"All power is given to thee in heaven and on earth," so that "at the command of Mary all obey—even God . . . and thus . . . God has placed the whole church . . . under the domination of Mary."[13]

Mary is "the advocate of the whole human race; fit for this office, for she can do what she wills with God; the most wise, for she knows all the means of appeasing him."[14]

"The whole Trinity, O Mary, gave thee a name . . . above

every other name, that at Thy name, every knee should bow, of things in heaven, on earth, and under the earth."[15] In these statements, Mary is given the attributes of deity. Since she is honored and prayed to around the world, she must be omnipresent, that is, everywhere simultaneously. If she can hear the prayers of millions of people around the world, given in dozens of different languages, she must be omniscient too. Obviously, she is more than just a special human being; she is doing what only God can do.

During the Middle Ages, when devotion to Mary reached its height, Christ was represented as a man of stern wrath, a strict judge who was waiting to sentence people to hell. Mary, on the other hand, was described as filled with love and mercy. As Ligouri says in his book, if God is angry with a sinner and Mary takes him under her protection, "she withholds the avenging arm of her Son and saves him." Thus, in a pinch, Mary is preferred to Christ. After all, the reasoning goes, what son would refuse the request of his mother?

To avoid the charge of idolatry, the Roman church has distinguished three kinds of honor or worship. *Latria* is the supreme worship that is given to God alone; *dulia* is a secondary kind of veneration given to saints and angels; and *hyperdulia* is a higher kind of veneration given to the Virgin Mary. These distinctions, however, are not always recognized by the common worshiper. Since Mary is given praise, and is thought of as having the attributes of deity, it is difficult to keep these three forms of worship in proper prospective. The practice, if not the theory, fosters idolatry.

If there should still be any doubt that Mary has been exalted as high as Christ, read the words of Pope Pius XII at the time of the coronation of Mary's statue at Fatima: "Mary is indeed worthy to receive honor and might and glory. She is exalted to hypostatic union with the Blessed Trinity. . . . Her kingdom is as great as her Son's and God's.

. . . Mary's kingdom is identical with the kingdom of God."[16]

But Pope Pius spoke those words in 1946. Far reaching changes have taken place in Rome since then, so we must compare the past with more recent pronouncements.


## Recent Catholic Beliefs

The doctrine of Mary sharply divides Catholics and Protestants. Since Catholic theologians themselves candidly admit that the characteristics and works ascribed to her are not found in the New Testament, there is no need to debate this doctrine from a scriptural point of view.

Two other questions come to mind: (1) Given the reforms of Vatican II, has the doctrine of Mary been modified sufficiently so that it no longer should be an obstacle to Christian unity, and (2) do such traditions actually detract from the gospel or should we dismiss them as harmless folklore?

To answer both questions, we turn to the documents of Vatican II. One of the purposes of this Council that met in 1962 was consciously to make the doctrines of Rome more palatable to Protestants, who are no longer regarded by the Catholic church as heretics but "separated brethren." Does the council either revoke or tone down the doctrine of Mary to make it more acceptable to New Testament theology?

On the very first day of the council, October 11, 1962, Pope John XXIII declared that the assembled delegates were met together "under the auspices of the virgin Mother of God" and he concluded with a prayer to Mary. Later the delegates would be more specific regarding the place of Mary in the church.[17]

But what does Vatican II actually teach about Mary? To be sure, the approved document does say that she is one with all human beings in her need for salvation. But yet, the council agrees that she was entirely holy and free from all stain of sin, "fashioned by the Holy Spirit into a kind of new substance and new creature." Having consented to the Lord's request given through the angel, she "served the mystery of redemption. Because of her obedience, she became the cause of salvation for herself and the whole human race. She cooperates with her Son in the saving of souls."

Notice carefully that her role in salvation has not diminished. According to the council, the blessed Virgin is appropriately called by the titles of Advocate, Auxiliatrix, Adjutrix, and Mediatrix. She is united with her Son, the Redeemer, and with his singular graces and offices. "Hence when she is preached and venerated, she summons the faithful to her Son and his sacrifice, and to love for the Father." And of course the faithful should pray to her.

Once again the council ascribed the attributes of Christ to Mary. She is the one who "gave life to the world." She is the model of the church, and those who "strive to increase in holiness . . . raise their eyes to Mary who shines forth to the whole community of the elect as a model of the virtues." And although the Bible teaches that Christ alone was without sin, the council affirmed that Mary was "entirely holy and free from all stain of sin" and in keeping with the teaching of past generations, she is the "Mediatrix," and by her cooperation in human salvation, there was a 'union of the Mother with the Son in the work of salvation."

These words are basically a summary of the doctrines already discussed in this chapter. None is denied. None is omitted.

The council does warn that preachers and teachers are to avoid the falsity of exaggeration of Mary on the one hand and the excess of narrow-mindedness on the other. And we are told that the work of Mary toward men in no way diminishes the unique work of Christ.

Observers of the council have pointed out that such

admonitions are not new; they have been given many times in the past. As Philip Edgcumbe Hughes says about such statements, "Protestations of scriptural orthodoxy have a hollow ring when they are used to justify teachings manifestly alien to the evangelical doctrines of Scripture. Besides, as has already been shown, the modern popes bear a heavy responsibility for the encouragement of the unbiblical exaggerations of the cult of Mary."[18]

The faithful are explicitly exhorted that the "cult, especially the liturgical cult, of the blessed Virgin be generously fostered" and that "practices and exercises of devotion toward her be treasured as recommended by the teaching authority of the church in the course of the centuries, and those decrees in earlier times regarding the veneration of the images of Christ, the blessed Virgin and the saints be religiously observed."

One might ask why the church would ratify this teaching, which is so antithetical to the Bible and the "separated brethren" it is committed to reach. A clue to this question is found by realizing that the doctrine of Mary embodies the essence of the Catholic teaching about salvation. It is one doctrine that cannot logically be modified.

For the Catholic church, salvation is a cooperative effort between God and man. Man contributes to his own justification by a proper disposition, such as good works, penances, and by faithful attendance in Mass. Thus, to quote Hughes, "This human potential is symbolized in a concrete manner in the person of Mary, free from the taint of sin, collaborating in redemption—without whose consent and cooperation, indeed our redemption would not have been effected—and exalted to the heights of divinity as queen-mother of heaven, there to intercede with a mother's compassionate heart and turn aside the displeasure of a less than indulgent Mediator."[19]

Mary as a co-redeemer symbolizes the belief that salvation is a cooperative effort between man and God. The famous Swiss theologian, Karl Barth, agrees that the doctrine of Mary is symbolic of what he calls the basic error of Rome. "In the doctrine of Mary is disclosed the one heresy of the Roman Catholic church which explains all the rest," he writes, for "Mary is the principle, type and essence of the human nature cooperating with God in redemption."[20]

Though many changes in theory and practice within the Catholic church have occurred, the doctrine of Mary is apparently nonnegotiable. She is the prototype of salvation; she represents man in his efforts to reach the favor of God.

### The Bible or Tradition?

Most churches have traditions; that is, they practice their religion according to forms. Often these forms have been handed down from previous generations. Some traditions are quite harmless; they do not detract from the centrality of Christ nor do they have doctrinal content.

But tradition that is accepted on an equal par with revelation deserves careful scrutiny. Pope John Paul affirmed "both Scripture and tradition must be accepted and honored with equal feelings of devotion and reverence." Tradition is serious business.

When the disciples were criticized for neglecting the Jewish traditions, Christ did not trivialize the encounter but used it to speak a word about tradition. He quoted Isaiah as saying, "But in vain do they worship Me, teaching as doctrines the precepts of men" (Mark 7:7).

Christ isn't finished yet. He adds his own commentary on tradition: "Neglecting the commandment of God, you hold to the tradition of men. . . . You nicely set aside the commandment of God in order to keep your tradition" (vv. 8-9).

Why such a distaste for tradition? It nullifies the commands of God by focusing attention in the wrong direction and therefore causes individuals to have misplaced faith. You cannot argue, as some do, that truth can be successfully mixed with tradition without compromising the message. To return to the subject of Mary: If she is but an ordinary human being, she is neither qualified nor able to hear the prayers of the faithful. All of the adoration directed toward her has been futile and even more seriously, has detracted from Christ, who alone is presented in the New Testament as the Savior of the world. If, on the other hand, she is a co-redeemer, then salvation is not wholly of the Lord. And if she is to be prayed to, then Christ's teaching about prayer in the New Testament must be modified.

Time and again, we shall have to return to the question of authority. Is it Scripture or tradition? The doctrine of Mary in the Roman Catholic church stands as a reminder that it cannot be both.

## Notes

1. Loraine Boettner, *Roman Catholicism* (Philadelphia: The Presbyterian and Reformed Publishing Co., 1962), 136.
2. Ludwig Ott, *Fundamentals of Catholic Dogma* (St. Louis: B. Herder Book Co., 1955), 199.
3. Ibid.
4. Ibid., 203.
5. Ibid., 208.
6. Ibid., 213.
7. Ibid., 214.
8. St. Alphonsus de Liguori, *The Glories of Mary* (Brooklyn: Redemptorist Fathers, 1931), 153.
9. Ibid.
10. Ibid., 130.
11. Ibid., 160.
12. Ibid., 170.
13. Ibid., 181.
14. Ibid., 198.
15. Ibid., 260.
16. Philip Edgcumbe Hughes, "The Council and Mary." *Christianity Today,* 8 Dec. 1967, 7.
17. Quotations from S. J. Walter Abbott, ed., *The Documents of Vatican II* (New York: Guild Press, 1966), 87-96.

18. Hughes, 9.
19. Ibid.
20. David Wells, *Revolution in Rome* (Downers Grove, Ill.: InterVarsity Press, 1972), 136-137.

# FOUR

# Was Peter the First Pope?

Christ's words to Peter, "Thou art Peter, and upon this rock I will build my church" (kjv), have caused a storm of controversy that has not abated throughout the centuries. Roman Catholicism claims these words prove that Peter was given supremacy over the other apostles and that this honor is transferred to the popes of the Roman Catholic church. And by inference, when the pope speaks from the chair of Peter, that is *ex cathedra,* he is infallible.

The authority of the pope is no longer taken as seriously by Catholics today as it once was. When he speaks about the evil of birth control or the sin of divorce, his words are often disregarded by many Catholics, especially in the United States. Today many who consider themselves good Catholics disagree with the pope about the role of women in the church and even abortion. But the official Roman Catholic teaching regarding the authority of the church in such matters still stands.

How did the idea of the papacy arise and why?

## Early Beginnings

A good place to start the discussion is to go back to the year A.D. 452, when Attila the Hun led his cavalry up the

Danube River with the intent of conquering the western half of the Roman Empire. A sudden raid over the Alps brought him into northern Italy. On toward Rome he marched until he was met by a Roman delegation, imploring him to leave. He was about to ignore them when he heard that Leo, the bishop of Rome, was among the group, representing the Roman emperor. Man to man, they faced each other, a foreign king and a ruling pope. According to some historians, Attila already had made up his mind that he could sustain no further conquests because of the deterioration of his army over the long marches. At any rate, he agreed to Leo's request that the capital be spared. That gave the bishop of Rome new stature not only as a religious leader but as a politician as well.

What does this have to do with the development of the papacy? Leo, known in history as Leo the Great, made much of the growing belief that the words of Christ to Peter, "Thou art Peter, and upon this rock I will build my church," were applicable to the bishop of Rome. This gave him the stature and authority he needed to rule.

But why should the bishop of Rome be granted this honor? After all, the church began in Jerusalem, and other important congregations existed in places such as Antioch in Syria and Ephesus.

But keep in mind that Rome was the capital of the Roman Empire. It was a city of political power and influence, a city where the early believers established a strong Christian church. Some estimates put the number of believers in Rome at thirty thousand. In the West, both the church and the city had no rival.

What is more, early Christian writers referred to Peter and Paul as having founded the church in Rome. Thus the idea arose that the bishop of Rome was in the succession of the apostles.

Then we must understand something of the structure of the church. Bishops arose in different parts of the country, but occasionally they met together for councils and to discuss church problems. As might be expected, the bishops from more important churches exerted more influence in these meetings. Some bishops thus began to exercise authority over certain geographical areas. The smaller churches had priests who in turn reported to the bishop. Thus, Rome grew in authority and power.

Finally, it all came to a head. After Constantine became the emperor in A.D. 312, he decided to move the capital of the Roman Empire to "the New Rome," namely Constantinople, a city he named after himself. Thus political power shifted from the west to the east. (Greece is in the east and represents an approximate dividing line between east and west.) When Constantine orchestrated the famous council of 325, it was held in Nicaea, just a few miles from Constantinople (see chapter 1).

Rivalry between the two cities developed. One day the emperor of Constantinople called a general council, just as Constantine had done. However, he invited bishops from the eastern part of the empire but ignored the bishop of Rome. The council took care of some theological matters but also stated that the bishop of Constantinople would be next to the bishop of Rome in authority because Constantinople was "the New Rome."

Meanwhile, back in "Old Rome," this statement was interpreted as a challenge to the authority of the Roman bishop. So, at a synod the next year in Rome, the western bishops asserted, "The Holy Roman church takes precedence over the other churches, not on the grounds of any synodal decisions, but because it was given the primacy by the words of our Lord and Redeemer in the Gospel when he said: 'Thou art Peter, and upon this rock I will build my church.' "

That was the theological climate into which Leo came. Politically, Rome was beginning to wane, and thus the old argument of the supremacy of the church of Rome because of Rome's power and influence carried less weight. But it didn't matter. Rome could now claim its superiority on the primacy of Peter alone. And because of the political deterioration of the city, the bishop was able to exercise more power.

Leo was well aware of the exalted position he had inherited. Thus, on the day he was installed, he affirmed that his new office extolled "the glory of the blessed Apostle Peter . . . in whose chair his power lives on and his authority shines forth." Christ promised to build his church on Peter, and this is the fulfillment of his words. Leo was a good preacher and organizer. He took many of the principles of Roman government and applied them to the church. Church organization was standardized throughout the empire.

Though Leo had been successful in staving off an attack by Attila the Hun, he could not stave off the Vandals who attacked Rome in A.D. 455. At the city gate, Leo met Gaiseric, the king of the Vandals, who had brought his troops just north of the Tiber River. Leo pled for mercy, but the Vandals ransacked Rome for fourteen days. They plundered palaces, took political prisoners and even members of the aristocracy for political ransom. With their ships loaded with treasures and people, the Vandals sailed for Carthage.

Pope Leo gave comfort to the people and thanksgiving to God. Because of his intercession with the king, a general massacre was avoided and most of the churches were spared. He invited the people to acknowledge God as the one who softened the heart of the barbarians. Bruce Shelley in his survey of church history says that Leo made no reference to himself and he did not have to, though he had saved Rome for a second time. "He had assumed the old heathen title *Pontifex Maximus,* the high priest of religion throughout the empire, and everyone understood. Leo, not the emperor, had shouldered the responsibility of the Eternal City. Peter had come to power."[1]

Jumping ahead several centuries, we look again at the rivalry that developed between the bishop of Rome and the bishop of Constantinople. The two segments of the church continued to drift further apart. Centuries went by until one day in 1054, just as a service was about to begin in the church of Holy Wisdom in Constantinople, two representatives of the church of Rome appeared and placed a papal bull (an official edict from the pope) on the altar. The pope of Rome was officially excommunicating the bishop of Constantinople. However, the bishop of Constantinople was unmoved. The bull was eventually dropped in the street when a deacon of the church urged the Roman delegation to take it back. Thus, the eastern block of Christendom separated itself from Rome. This explains the existence of the Eastern Orthodox church, which affirms much of Catholicism (though with important differences) but refuses to accept the authority of the pope.

## The Popes and Political Power

As we have noted, Leo the Great was the first Roman pontiff to exercise political as well as spiritual power. But he was not the last. To understand the papacy, we must realize that religion became such a powerful force during the Middle Ages that it gave the popes the ability to dominate the political as well as the spiritual realm. And in the search for unity, the popes took the lead.

With the rise of Pope Gregory the Great (A.D. 540–606) the papacy led the way in the standardization of worship and liturgy. Gregory renounced great wealth and served the people in humility. He called himself the "servant of the servants of God."

Under his leadership, the church expanded both in power and territory. When the Lombards attacked Rome, it was Gregory who recruited an army to defend Rome. Once again, spiritual and political power were united in one man.

Gregory is best known for his chant that standardized

the worship in the churches. He also encouraged the growing tendency to think of the Mass as a sacrifice of Christ's body and blood. In his day, he was loved for his relevant messages and commentary on the Book of Job. His handbook on pastoral theology entitled *The Book of Pastoral Rule* had a great impact throughout the empire.

He believed in purgatory as a place where souls were purified before they entered heaven. His theology was not only derived from the teachings of the New Testament and the church fathers, but also from prevalent superstitions about relics and prayers to the saints. He believed that the Mass had value for the dead as well as the living. Salvation, he taught, was obtained by both faith and good works.

Gregory is usually thought of as the first of the medieval popes. His work set the direction of the church theologically, liturgically, and politically for years to come.

Years later, in 799, Pope Leo III was leading a procession through the streets of Rome when he was pulled off his horse and taken to a Greek monastery. The supporters of the previous pope charged him with perjury and adultery. But his supporters rescued him and brought him back to Saint Peter's Basilica. He realized that if he was to rule, he would need to fill a political void by crowning an emperor who could give him protection. So he appealed to the king of the Franks, Charles the Great.

On Christmas Day in the year 800, Charles came to Saint Peter's for worship. On that occasion the pope approached Charles with a crown in his hand and placed it on his head. At last, the disintegrating Roman Empire would be unified once more. The fact that the emperor had been crowned by the pope demonstrated the strength of papal power.

Charles the Great had the military power to crush his enemies. He desired to see Christianity the dominant religious influence within the empire. He believed that the souls of men corresponded to the church; man's body to the state. Thus the church rules over the spirits of men and the state over their bodies. The pope and emperor have to support one another in their God-given duties as they expand their power for the good of mankind.

Charlemagne, as Charles the Great was called, was very much in charge. He extended Christianity throughout the Roman Empire and restored law and order. He led about fifty campaigns to end anarchy within his kingdom and expand his borders. He also advanced culture and education.

## Pope and Emperor Clash

There were times when the papacy failed in its attempts to control political leaders. In the eleventh century a dispute arose about whether or not political authorities had the power to make church appointments. In Germany the feudal lords and kings had grasped enough power to control the church.

When Pope Gregory VII came to power in 1073, he insisted that the spiritual power was supreme over the political rulers. He threatened to excommunicate any person who derived his authority to minister in church from civil rulers. This brought him into sharp conflict with the emperor, Henry IV. The pope accused Henry of simony (buying or selling church offices). So Henry was summoned to appear before the pope. Instead Henry called a synod to declare the pope unfit for office. In retaliation, Pope Gregory excommunicated Henry and absolved all his subjects from their allegiance to the emperor.

Henry decided that he had better make amends or lose his power, so he appeared before the Pope in January 1077 at Canossa, a castle in the mountains of Italy. The emperor was dressed in the clothes of a penitent, but was forced to stand for three days barefoot in the snow, begging forgiveness. Finally, in Gregory's words, "We loosed

the chain of the anathema and at length received him . . .
into the lap of the Holy Mother Church." Once again
papal supremacy was affirmed. Later Henry consolidated
his power and returned, this time taking Gregory captive.

As the centuries progressed, for the most part papal
power continued to increase, strengthened by the weak
political leadership in Europe. The former glory of the
emperor was replaced by the religious leadership of the
popes. They not only were recognized as spiritual leaders
but became the acknowledged head of kings and princes.
The church, it was believed, had two swords, the Word of
God and the sword of steel. The temporal political power
was to be used to fulfill the will of the universal church.
Thus the state would aid in the salvation of man. The idea
that political unity is possible with religious diversity had
simply not entered the minds of medieval rulers.


## The Crusades

In 1095, Pope Urban II proclaimed the first crusade to
liberate the Holy Land from the Muslim Turks. He urged
Christians to take up the cross and to win spiritual blessings as well as the territory for themselves. He promised
that those who went would be given forgiveness for all of
their past sins. If a person could not go, he could make a
financial contribution and send a substitute. He too
would be forgiven for past sins.

More than five thousand made the journey and captured
the Holy City of Jerusalem. The Turks were shot with
arrows, their heads cut off. One witness, putting it all into
a theological perspective, wrote, "Indeed it was a just and
splendid judgment of God that this place should be filled
with the blood of the unbelievers, since it had suffered so
long from their blasphemies." Obviously, it was the pope,
not the emperor, who united the empire against the threat
of Muslim power.

Pope Innocent III ( 1198–1216) was an able administrator who said that the Vicar of Christ was less than God but beyond man. He told the princes of Europe that the papacy was like the sun, while kings were like the moon, whose power was derived from the sun. Under his leadership the power of the papacy reached its zenith.

The pope was able to keep the princes in line with the threat of excommunication, in which case a person was immediately disqualified from all offices and would not even receive a Christian burial. If the king of a country did not obey the pope, his whole territory would be placed under the *interdict.* All public worship in the area was suspended except baptism and extreme unction. Thus, the political authorities had to fall in line or be removed from power.

## The Papacy in Disarray

The power of the papacy, however, ran into some stiff resistance in the fourteenth century. Pope Boniface locked horns with Edward I of England and Philip of France because they began to tax the clergy in their realms. Boniface issued *unam sanctam,* the most extreme assertion of papal power possible. He declared that every human being was to be subject to the Roman pontiff. Philip responded by attempting to bring the pope to trial in France and had his men capture the pontiff while he vacationed in a summer home. He was imprisoned for several days and died in humiliation a few weeks later.

Undoubtedly, Philip had scored a victory. And when a successor to Boniface died after a brief reign, the cardinals, in 1305, elected a Frenchman, Clement V, as pope. But he never came to Rome, preferring rather to reign from Avignon in southern France. That began a seventy-two-year period in which six successive popes, all of French origin, ruled from France rather than the Eternal City. Historians have dubbed it the "Babylonian Captivity" of the church.

This move was bitterly resented, especially in Germany and Italy. These countries refused to support the papacy, so the French popes raised money by fees and taxes for ecclesiastical privileges. Whenever a bishop was appointed, his first year's salary would go to the papacy. Indulgences were sold, conferring spiritual benefits ranging from the forgiveness of sins to protection in war.

When at last the papacy moved back to Rome in 1377, the cardinals, many of whom were French, yielded to pressure and elected an Italian pope, Urban VI. But less than six months later, they regretted their decision because of his disdain for them. They retaliated by saying they had been forced into choosing him because of the pressure of Rome. Thus they declared their own action invalid. They chose a new pope, Clement VII. He decided that he would move to Avignon.

Meanwhile the deposed pope, Urban VI, responded by appointing a new college of cardinals and continuing his rule from Rome. This was the beginning of what is known in history as the "Great Schism," which lasted thirty-nine years. Two popes ruled simultaneously, each claiming the power to excommunicate the other. The people had to choose which one they would follow. Northern Italy, most of Germany, Scandinavia, and England followed the Roman pope; France, Spain, Scotland, and southern Italy were loyal to the pope at Avignon.

In 1409, a group of cardinals from the rival factions met to resolve the conflict. They deposed both of the present popes and named a new one, Alexander V. But neither of the other two popes accepted the decision of the council. So the church now had three popes, each claiming to be the legitimate successor to Peter, calling the others Antichrist, and selling indulgences to make enough money to fight against the others.

In 1414, the emperor called an assembly in the city of Constance. Delegates attended on the basis of geographical representation and had enough power to get one of the three popes to step down and depose the other two. They elected a new pope, Martin V, and eventually the other two accepted the reality of the situation and relinquished their papal authority.

The schism was over, but a new problem emerged. Pope Martin V repudiated all the acts of the council that elected him except one—namely their decision to elect him as pope. His reason: by electing a new pope and deposing the others, the Council of Constance was, in effect, affirming that a council had authority over the pope. This the new pope would not tolerate.

Thus, the pope was again considered supreme. As Shelley says, once again he could not make up his mind whether he was the successor of Peter or Caesar.

## The Infallibility of the Pope

As the papacy grew in influence, so did the expected allegiance to its teachings. As Peter was first among the apostles, so was the bishop of Rome first among the bishops. In the year 1647, Pope Innocent X rejected as heretical the idea that Peter and Paul were joint heads of the church. The fact that Paul "withstood Peter to the face" (Gal. 2:11) does not negate Peter's supreme position; indeed, Rome took the view that Paul reprimanded Peter precisely because Peter's high authority in the church necessitated that he be corrected.

The infallibility of the pope was reiterated at the first Vatican Council in 1870. It declared that "if anyone denies that . . . Blessed Peter has perpetual successors in his Primacy over the Universal Church, let him be anathema."[2] The council also went on to affirm that the pope possesses full and supreme power of jurisdiction over the whole church, not merely in faith and morals, but also in church discipline and in the government of the church.

Specifically, this means that the pope has more power than all the bishops together. In fact, to quote the words of the Roman Catholic theologian Ludwig Ott, the pope possesses "supreme power in the Church, that is, there is no jurisdiction possessing a greater or equally great power. The power of the pope transcends both the power of each individual bishop and also of all the other bishops together. The bishops collectively (apart from the pope), therefore, are not equal to or superior to the pope." To quote Ott again, "Thus the pope can rule independently on any matter which comes under the sphere of the church's jurisdiction without the concurrence of other bishops or of the rest of the church."[3]

This doctrine received strong opposition from within the church itself. One leading theologian, Dollinger, who had taught theology for forty-seven years, was excommunicated in 1871 because of his opposition to this dogma. He correctly noted that such a belief abdicated the need for councils and the bishops, since they cannot override a papal decision. Regarding the bishops, he wrote, "If they wish to confirm a papal decision . . . this would be bringing lanterns to aid the noonday sun." Thus the council, in giving the pope complete jurisdiction and the gift of infallibility, made it impossible to judge his teachings by the Bible. When the pope speaks *ex cathedra,* he can supersede the Scriptures. All protests are silenced.

Though there is no direct historical evidence that Peter ever was in Rome, the church believes that he died there and the original Saint Peter's Basilica was built over his tomb.

What of the primacy of Peter, the transfer of his authority to the bishop of Rome, and the infallibility of the pope? Is this the teaching of the New Testament? Or are there other valid reasons to believe these doctrines?

## The Papacy and the New Testament

When Christ said to Peter, "Thou art Peter and upon this rock I will build my church," he evidently intended that

there be a play on words—the word *Peter* means *rock.*
But it should not escape our notice that there are two
separate Greek words used. "Thou art Peter [Petros] and
upon this [petra] I will build my church." Since *petra* is a
slab of rock, Christ may have had himself in mind. Elsewhere in the New Testament he is spoken of as the foundation of the church.

However, let us, for the sake of the discussion, say that
he did mean Peter. Roman Catholic theologians would
affirm that the church is based upon both Christ and
Peter. But even if this be granted, three questions arise.
First, is there any evidence in the Bible that Peter's authority is transferable? Second, is there anything to suggest
that this power has been transferred to the bishops of
Rome? And third, is there anything in the New Testament
to suggest that Peter was infallible in his pronouncements
and that this gift has also been conferred upon the Roman
bishops?

Ludwig Ott, the Catholic theologian, is again in the
unenviable position of having to admit that the primacy of
Peter is not expressly stated in the words of Christ, but it
flows as an inference from the nature and purpose of the
papacy. As for the belief that Peter's power is transferable
or that it has been conferred on the bishops of Rome, no
Scripture is cited.

And what about infallibility? Ott admits that the church
fathers did not speak of the infallibility of the pope but
implied it in some of their statements. As for Scripture, he
appeals to the fact that Christ gave Peter the authority of
binding and loosing (Matt. 16:18-20). But we should
notice that this was not given to Peter alone but to all the
apostles in Matthew 18:18 and in John 20:23. Peter was
given the keys to the kingdom because he was chosen to
preach the gospel to the Jews and Gentiles (Acts 2, 10,
15). But the text does not mention that this privilege was
transferable.

That Peter was fallible is quite clear from Galatians, in

which Paul said that he rebuked Peter publicly for compromising the purity of the gospel. Under pressure from some Jews, Peter lapsed back into the Old Testament dietary practices. Paul saw this as inconsistent with the gospel that rejects such distinctions and offers salvation to Gentiles and Jews alike. Paul wrote, "I opposed him to his face, because he stood condemned" (Gal. 2:11).

In the New Testament the highest position of leadership is the elder or bishop (the words are used interchangeably in many passages). But nowhere does one bishop exercise authority over other churches, much less that one should claim authority over all Christendom. The elders (bishops) of each local church are responsible only for their own members. The danger of investing undue authority in one man is that when he errs, other churches err with him.

Though a council may be called, it is not binding over other churches. For example, the first church council met in Jerusalem and was led by James (not Peter, even though he was present); yet the conclusions were presented to the other churches as those that "seemed good," not ones that had to be followed regardless of whether the other churches agreed with them or not. What is clear is that the conclusion of any council must be tested by the Scripture before a decision is made to follow it (Acts 15:22-29).

Can unity be maintained without one earthly head? Protestants say Christ is the only head of the church and that unity should be based on the doctrines of Scripture alone.

The writings of the New Testament that speak most clearly about the headship of Christ and the equal authority of all believers before God are those written by Peter. He presented Christ as the chief cornerstone (1 Pet. 2:6). With equal clarity he taught that every believer is a priest before God (1 Pet. 2:4-7). As for the position of elders or bishops, he admonishes that they "shepherd the flock of God . . . not under compulsion, but voluntarily, according to the will of God; and not for sordid gain, but with eagerness; nor yet as lording it over those allotted to your charge, but proving to be examples to the flock" (1 Pet. 5:2-3). He did not foresee one bishop extending his authority over one church, much less over *all* the churches. Only Christ has such authority. Papal claims must be evaluated in the light of Peter's own pronouncements.

### Notes

1. Bruce Shelley, *Church History in Plain Language* (Waco, Texas: Word Books, 1982), 158.
2. Ludwig Ott, *Fundamentals of Catholic Dogma* (St. Louis: B. Herder Books Co., 1954), 282.
3. Ibid., 285.

# FIVE

# Justification: By Faith, Sacraments, or Both?

Life's most important question can be phrased in various ways. In the Old Testament Job asked, "How can a man be in the right before God?" The young ruler confronted Christ with, "What shall I do to obtain eternal life?" And the Philippian jailor in terror asked, "What must I do to be saved?"

Sadly, though we have had the New Testament for almost twenty centuries, Christendom still gives an unclear answer to this question. Yet our destiny in heaven or hell depends on the correctness of the answer.

The teaching of the New Testament on this point is quite uncomplicated. At least one hundred times we read that faith in Christ is the means by which a sinner is declared forgiven and gladly received by the Almighty. When Christ died on the cross, one of his last words was *tetelestai,* translated, "It is finished" (John 19:30). In Greek the word was used in commercial transactions and, written across a bill, it meant, "Paid in full." Christ's death was totally sufficient for all who put their trust in him *alone.*

Two implications follow. First, we are not saved by human effort. If Christ paid the full and final price for salvation, then we are not received on the basis of our merit. "For by grace you have been saved through faith; and that not of yourselves, it is the gift of God; not as a result of works, that no one should boast" (Eph. 2:8-9). Salvation is, above all, a free gift.

Doesn't this mean we can be saved and then live as sinfully as we please? This question is often asked by those who think that works *must* be involved in salvation. Even if Christ made the down payment, we must keep up the installments. But the answer is yes, once we have received the free gift, it is ours forever even if it is abused. But let us not overlook the fact that the change God brings about as the result of faith is so radical that our desires are changed. God moves into our lives and begins the process of renovation. Spiritual growth is a whole separate story.

That leads me to a second implication. God works directly in a human being by the Holy Spirit through the truth of the Scriptures. There need be no human inter-mediaries such as a priest nor any rituals. The miracle of the new birth happens directly at the moment of saving faith. Dozens of such stories are found on the pages of the New Testament. Whether it is Lydia the seller of purple, "whose heart the Lord opened," or the Ethiopian eunuch, or the thief on the cross, those who believed were saved directly in response to the gift of faith.

During the first three centuries of church history, the doctrine of salvation by grace through faith was preached with varying degrees of clarity. In some cases faith was indeed presented as the sole requirement for salvation, but in other instances works and baptism were tied into the gift of grace. Even the so-called apostolic fathers (who were called such because they evidently knew the apos-tles themselves) sometimes stressed the need for works for salvation, or at least as necessary to maintain one's salvation after it had been freely received.

Early on, there were references to sacramentalism, the belief that ordinances such as baptism and Communion were necessary to salvation. For example, Hermas (ca. 100), one of the apostolic fathers, wrote, "There is no other repentance than this, that we go down into the water and receive the forgiveness of our past sins."[1] Ignatius, bishop of Antioch (ca. 100), another of the apostolic fathers, spoke of the benefit of Communion. To him the Eucharist was "the medicine of immortality, an antidote that we might not die, but live in Jesus Christ forever."[2] And in what is called the Letter of Clement (the author is unknown), eternal life is spoken of as granted at baptism; and even after that, purity of life is needed to guarantee that one will enter into heaven. Barnabas (not to be confused with the Barnabas of the New Testament) also wrote that the believer enters the possession of the blessings of redemption though baptism.

As time went on, sacramentalism did not die. Baptism and Communion were believed by some as efficacious in taking away sin. Once this premise was accepted, it seemed reasonable that babies should be baptized—why should they be denied the benefits of grace? After all, they were guilty of original sin. Next, it was argued that they should be given Communion, too. As we shall see in a future chapter, these views arose particularly in North Africa during the second and third centuries.

Of course, these views were by no means unanimous. Polycarp, a personal friend of the Apostle John, taught that we are saved by faith alone. Works follow salvation but do not contribute to the gift of eternal life. Consistent with the teaching of John's Gospel, Polycarp taught that eternal life was given directly in response to saving faith; nothing is said about the need for sacraments. Reinhold Seeberg, who has written a comprehensive history of Christian doctrine, says that the apostolic fathers did not have a systematic grasp of the doctrine of salvation because they show little evidence of having understood Paul's epistles. They are acquainted with the writings of Peter and James but not the doctrinal gist of Romans.[3]

So there were some who opposed the view that salvation was mediated through external rituals. Indeed, it is probable that sacramentalism may not have had such a firm hold during the Middle Ages were it not for the coming of Constantine and his impact on the understanding of the church. At any rate, his leadership led to the acceptance of sacramentalism throughout the empire.

## The Rise of Sacramentalism

With the coming of Constantine, sacramentalism shifted into high gear. From now on the church would be used for political purposes, and *the sacraments would be the means by which the church would control the lives of those who lived in the Roman Empire.* Salvation was no longer thought of as a personal relationship with God but a proper relationship with the church.

Think of the power that was now vested in the church! It held the keys to heaven and hell. It could give grace or withhold it. To say that one had made his peace with God outside of the church was to speak heresy. As sacramentalism grew, so did the liturgy that accompanied it. Practices not found in the New Testament arose to accompany the exalted view given to these rituals.

Despite Augustine's clear understanding of the depravity of man and the need for grace, he also stressed a need for the sacraments in salvation. Baptism, he taught, impresses on man a special character. Also, he further clouded the issue by teaching that works have no merit before the gift of faith is exercised, but as a result of the renewal of the heart, works result that are meritorious. As one writer, speaking of Augustine, put it, "Fundamentally, therefore, grace merely serves the purpose of making it possible for man once more to merit salvation."[4]

Augustine became involved in an important controversy about the sacraments. The Donatists, led by their leader Donatus, argued that sacraments only had validity if the priest who administered them was leading a righteous life. Augustine saw quite clearly that this would put the salvation of the masses in jeopardy, since no one could be sure that a given priest was actually living a worthy life. So he asserted that the sacraments were a gift from God and the moral condition of the administrator could not detract from their value. Indeed, the sacraments would have value even if administered by thieves and robbers.

Augustine was caught in a curious problem. He had to oppose the Donatists even though he was forced to conclude that their sacraments were valid—after all, *all* sacraments are valid. Yet he went on to distinguish between the sacrament itself and the effects of the sacrament, hoping to find reasons to oppose the Donatists. As for baptism, Augustine said that it could not be repeated; therefore, it would never lose its force. Yet, he also said that only when a person receives grace in other ways does baptism become effectual.

The problem of the intrinsic value of the nonrepeatable sacraments of baptism, confirmation, and holy orders later occupied much discussion in sacramental theology. Do these rituals still have value even for those who apostatize and leave the church? And if such people return, why do some sacraments not have to be repeated? Remember, the sacraments were said to have intrinsic validity regardless of the life of the priest. What is more, even the recipient did not need to have faith or a good inner motive to benefit from these means of grace.

Seeberg says in his discussion of Augustine, "A good inner motive is not required in the recipient by which he may merit grace by worthiness of fitness, but it sufficed that the recipient interpose no obstacle."[5] Basically, the church affirmed that the sacraments were of value to the recipient just as long as no mortal sin had been committed. If such were the case, this obstacle would have to be first removed by an act of perfect contrition.

The Donatists believed that the church should be pure;

that is, membership should be limited to believers. But Augustine, using Christ's parable about the wheat and the tares as a reference to the church (not the world), argued that unbelievers should be a part of its membership. This was based on his conception of the church as being inclusive of all of society.

Understandably, the temptation arose to build a network of sacraments, each of which would dispense a reservoir of grace to the penitent. Thus, during medieval times, the church progressively increased its control over the souls of men. And as the traditions grew, these were given the same status as the very words of Scripture. Eventually seven sacraments were fixed by Pope Eugene IV at the Council of Florentine in A.D. 1439.

Space forbids a detailed analysis of each one. Their basic presupposition was that *each sacrament dispensed grace, but no one sacrament had enough grace to save sinners.* Thus a person must take advantage of as many means of grace as are available to him. In the end the question will be whether one has accumulated enough grace to be saved.

This made the assurance of personal salvation impossible. It was difficult to calculate the amount of grace one had accumulated in comparison to the amount that God required. All that was left was the promise that eventually the church would be able to bring the sinner to heaven. For those who came up short on grace at death there was purgatory, a place where sinners would be purged from their sins at some future date. But to claim the assurance of heaven became the sin of presumption.

A second result was that the priests began to wield awesome power. The technical word for it is *sacerdotalism* (pronounced sac-er-do-tal-ism), the exaltation of the priests to the point of having divine powers. As the dispensers of grace, they have the right to exclude from heaven, or to include those who are submissive to their authority. As the Mass arose, it was believed that they had the authority to turn ordinary bread and wine into the body and blood of Christ. They were literally God's representatives on earth. Rather than accepting the New Testament teaching that all believers were priests, they went back to the Old Testament model of the priesthood where the Levites represented men to God and God to men.

What is the way of salvation in the Catholic church? It is through the church, but the church itself has a variety of requirements. Salvation is by grace, but grace involves many channels that the faithful will pursue. Thus, quest for eternal life is far from simple and often unclear.

## How It Works

Consider one of the sacraments, for example, to see how they were applied. Penance is the fourth sacrament and is defined in the Baltimore Catechism as "a sacrament by which sins committed after baptism are forgiven through the absolution of a priest."[6] But since the priest generally assigns some work for the penitent to do to gain absolution, the word frequently refers to the work itself. The belief is that God does not cancel the temporal punishment due because of sin, thus the sinner must supplement Christ's work by performing some good deed. The sinner is at the mercy of the priest who prescribes a proper penalty.

To be specific, if someone tells a lie and thus goes to confession, he examines his conscience and believes he has made a good confession. Yet there is a work he must do to remove the residual stain of the sin. Thus, the priest will likely require that he do a good deed, an act of penance.

The extent of the punishment often depends on the disposition of the priest. Today, in contrast to previous centuries, the penitent is usually assigned some easy task, such as reciting a number of "Hail Marys" or doing a kind deed. Whether or not he has a genuinely repentant spirit is not really at issue. *It is not his relationship with God that is really at stake as much as his relationship to the church.*

Closely related to penance is an indulgence, which is defined as "the remission, in whole or in part, of the temporal punishment due to sin. . . . A plenary indulgence is the full remission of the temporal punishment due to sin. . . . A partial indulgence is the remission of a part of the temporal punishment due to sin. . . . To gain an indulgence we must be in the state of grace (the result of a satisfactory confession to a priest) and perform the works enjoined."[7]

An indulgence is not a sacrament, but is the remission of temporal punishment *for sins that have already been forgiven.* It aids in the healing process and can also alleviate the sufferings of purgatory.

To understand this better we must remember that the church believed that there was a treasury of merit that had accumulated because some of the saints of the past had more righteousness than they needed to get to heaven. The church could draw on this reservoir for those who were spiritually needy. To quote the famous bishop Fulton Sheen, through these merits the "Church gives her penitents a fresh start. And the Church has tremendous spiritual capital, gained through centuries of penance, persecution, and martyrdom; many of her children prayed, suffered, and merited more than they needed for their own individual salvation. The Church took these superabundant merits and put them into the spiritual treasury, out of which repentant sinners can draw in times of spiritual depression."[8]

With the threat of purgatory hanging over their heads, the people of the Middle Ages were anxious to get indulgences that were guaranteed to shorten, if not cancel, their expected arrival in the fires of purgatory. But how could they get one, since they were granted only by the pope?

In A.D. 1096, at the Synod of Clermont, Pope Urban II promised a plenary indulgence, that is, one that covered all temporal punishment, for those who would participate in Crusades to the Holy Land. Three hundred years later, in 1477, Pope Sixtus IV declared that indulgences were not only valid for the living but also for the dead. Thus indulgences were sold to the populace for their relatives in purgatory.

Once the premise was accepted that the pope had the authority to grant indulgences, the door was now wide open for abuses. When Pope Leo X needed money to build Saint Peter's Cathedral in Rome, he let it be known that indulgences could be purchased to forgive the sins of the living and to release the souls of the dead. It was this opportunity for the church to make money that led Tetzel to come to the borders of Saxony to peddle indulgences.

## The Reformation

Luther's problem was in knowing how a sinful man could stand in the presence of a holy God. So he decided to pursue holiness. He resolutely began by practicing the counsels of perfection. Not only did he perform good deeds but he fasted and mortified the flesh. He laid on himself the vigils and prayers in excess of those stipulated. The problem was that he could never be sure that he had satisfied God at any point.

Confession was of some solace to him. He would search his memory to evaluate the motives he had for every act he performed. Sometimes for six hours he would confess his sins until his confessor became weary. Staupitz finally told him, "If you expect Christ to forgive you, come in with something to forgive—patricide, blasphemy, adultery—instead of these peccadilloes."[9] But Luther's question was not whether his sins were little or big but whether they had been confessed. He realized that one can even sin without being aware of it.

As historian Roland Bainton says, Luther arrived at an impasse. "Sins to be forgiven had to be confessed. To be confessed they had to be recognized and remembered. If they are not recognized and remembered, they cannot be confessed. If they are not confessed, they cannot be forgiven."[10]

During these struggles, Luther became aware that his problem was even more serious than he thought. It is not just that man commits sins, but he himself is inwardly defiled. To use a modern illustration of Luther's dilemma, confession was like trying to mop up the floor with the faucet running. There was not so much as a moment of assurance that one was fully right with God. *What Luther needed was an act of God that would take all his sins away, past, present, and future.*

Then the light dawned. Through his study of Paul's Epistle to the Romans, Luther learned that a man is justified by faith without the works of the law. Justification means that God *declares* a sinner to be righteous, even though he remains imperfect. For example, Paul wrote, "For what does the Scripture say? 'And Abraham believed God, and it was reckoned to him as righteousness' " (Rom. 4:3). That word *reckoned* is a legal term, often used when crediting money to someone's account. More specifically, Paul wrote, "But to the one who does not work, but believes in Him who justifies the ungodly, his faith is reckoned as righteousness" (Rom. 4:5).

Justification covers all sins, past, present, and future. Once a sinner is justified, it is not necessary for him to be able to remember all the sins he has committed. He is declared holy by God. The sinner who is thus received no longer owes God righteousness. He is fully and forever received. Because he is declared holy, God can make him an heir of God and a joint-heir with Christ.

Of course, it is true that Christians are told they must confess their sins even after having been justified (1 John 1:9). But this is necessary only to restore *fellowship* with

God; it is not necessary to reestablish the *legal* relationship with him. We stand before God, clothed in the righteousness of Christ even though we continue in sin. Little wonder Paul was charged with teaching *antinomianism,* the belief that one can misuse the grace of God to excuse sin! Whether this criticism is justified will be considered in a future chapter.

If justification means that God takes away all of a person's past and future sins forever, then assurance of heaven becomes possible. But if salvation is dependent on increments of grace given over a lifetime, assurance is beyond reach. To depend on the merit of Christ alone is to be assured of a fully adequate basis for forgiveness and acceptance.

To Luther's astonishment and delight, he had found the answer to his quest. He could stand before a holy God because of the complete and adequate merit of Christ. Of course this discovery, though new to Luther, was hardly new in the history of the church. The fact that it had to be rediscovered is a sad commentary on how far the church had drifted from the New Testament.

If justification is by faith alone without works, what place do works have in the Christian life? Now that the believer's relationship with God has been settled forever, he is free to serve the Lord with confidence and joy. The believer now does not do good works in order to be saved, but he does good because he already is saved. The good works are not meritorious in the sense that they can take away a single sin; rather they now flow from the new life that God has implanted in him.

## The Roman Catholic Response

At the Council of Trent in 1546, the Roman Catholic church officially responded to Martin Luther's insistence that a man can be justified by God on the basis of faith alone. The council acknowledged that all the works a man can do are solely because of the grace of God; but these works are part of the salvation process. Specifically, the following statement was condemned as anathema: "That the impious are justified by faith alone—if this means that nothing else is required by way of cooperation in the acquisition of the grace of justification, and that it is in no way necessary for a man to be prepared and disposed by the motion of his own will."[11] Also, the council affirmed that even after one was justified, works were necessary to maintain one's state of grace. All of the seven sacraments of the church were then defended.

The Catholic church, then, denied that faith alone was sufficient or that a person could be saved outside of the rituals of the church. Though there were some reforms, the basic sacramental system remained intact.

What about Catholicism today? For example, does the church still teach that such things as penance and indulgences grant increments of grace to the faithful? Even now, Roman Catholics who are in Saint Peter's Square when the pope delivers his traditional Christmas and Easter blessings have been offered a plenary indulgence, that is, that a person is freed from punishment in purgatory for sins. Since this indulgence is only valid for past sins, it is no guarantee for the future. But at least the recipient is brought up to date in his relationship with God.

In 1939, Pope Pius extended this benefit to radio listeners. In December of 1985, the Vatican announced that the people are now able to receive such an indulgence from their bishop's blessing via radio or TV if they are unable to hear him in person. Thus, the practice of granting indulgences is still faithfully practiced.

## Sacraments or Faith?

Sacramentalism stresses that salvation comes through the church's channels of grace. A related word *sacerdotalism*, refers to the exalted power of the priest in dispensing the grace of God. This view stands in stark contrast to justification by faith alone. Both views say that salvation is by grace, but they disagree sharply on the question of how grace is received.

The answers conflict. Which view is biblical?

Sacramentalism asks sinners to look to the church to be saved. It is through the church and its ordinances that God's grace is communicated to men. The church takes the place of God. As Benjamin Warfield, Princeton Seminary theologian of many years ago, wrote, "The question which is raised in sacerdotalism, in a word, is just whether it is God the Lord who saves us, or it is men acting in the name and clothed with the power of God, to whom we look for our salvation."[12] He added that if sacerdotalism is right, people are not saved or lost by divine appointment but by the natural working of secondary causes.

Warfield gave three objections to the sacramental or sacerdotal view of salvation. First, it separates the soul from direct contact with God and the Holy Spirit as the source of all gracious activity. The church stands between the soul and God. There is very little communion of the soul and God; the church takes care of the sinner's relationship with God for him.

The New Testament teaches that salvation involves not only the forgiveness of sins, but also the miracle of the new birth. Regeneration is nothing less than the creation of a new heart in the life of a sinner. This conversion changes his desires and results in a new life-style. Often this is overlooked when a sinner comes before a priest to find out what work he can do to atone for his sin. Rather than have his life changed by God, he begins to calculate just how much his sin costs him. If the price is not too high . . . if it just means going to Mass each week or to confession once or twice a year, there is no reason to repent personally and receive the forgiveness and life of God for himself. These matters take care of themselves as long as he is rightly related to the church.

Those who are converted out of sacramentalism usually

say that previously they did not know a personal relationship with God was possible. They had always only thought about whether they had covered all the bases by obedience to the requirements that the church prescribed. They didn't know that God works directly in the human heart.

Second, Warfield said that by interposing the church between the sinner and God, the personality of the Holy Spirit is diminished. Rather than believing that the Holy Spirit works according to his own will and purpose, he is thought of as working uniformly, whenever his activities are released by the church. Since the church is considered as the "storehouse of salvation," it is almost as if the saving grace of God is kept on tap and released at the will of the church. The Spirit moves according to the rituals of men. Remember, it is not even necessary for the priest to be living a good moral life for the sacraments to be valid. The ritual itself is intrinsically able to effect salvation.

The third difficulty is that salvation is no longer in the hands of God but in the hands of men. The Holy Spirit "goes where they convey him; he works when they release him for work; his operations wait for their permission; and apart from their direction and control he can work no salvation."[13] Those who ignore the sacraments are lost; those who accept them are saved. Because salvation is not in the hands of God but in the hands of men, the Catholic church teaches that there can be no salvation outside of the church. If we ask why one person is saved and not another, the answer is that some received the sacraments and others did not. The focus is on the sacraments, not personal faith in Christ.

To the sacramentalist, a baby who dies unbaptized will go to hell, or at least his eternal destiny is in doubt. So if the baby's life is in jeopardy, a priest is quickly called to perform the ritual. But he might be delayed and not arrive in time. Conceivably, the eternal abode of the child could be dependent on whether the priest is caught in a traffic jam. Of course the church, in facing such problems, appealed to purgatory and prayers for the dead to find a solution to the maze of complications created by the sacramental system. But salvation is still in the hands of men. If the parents do not follow through with these rituals the child will most probably be lost.

Contrast this with the teaching of the Bible, in which salvation is spoken of as the direct work of God in the human heart in response to saving faith. Since baptism and the Mass will be discussed in detail in following chapters, we need not discuss the New Testament interpretation of these sacraments here.

A contrast between the two approaches to salvation outlined in this chapter could be illustrated by a discussion I had with a Protestant who converted to the Catholic faith. A woman who joined in the conversation said that she would get to heaven because she had earned $1,200 for her church in a bake sale. When I asked her whether she would have anything else to offer God, she replied that she would depend on the grace of God. My Catholic friend approved of her answer with this parable:

A man came to the pearly gates and was asked by Saint Peter why he should be admitted into heaven. The man replied,

"My parents had me baptized."

Peter replied, "That's worth five points."

"I went to Mass once a week."

"That's twenty points."

"I went to confession twice a year."

"That's ten points."

"I had an honest business."

"That's five points."

With this the man became fearful, for he could think of no other merit he had accumulated, and he had only forty of the hundred points needed. But fortunately he remembered a sermon he had heard on grace so he quickly said,

"I'm depending on the grace of God."

To which Peter replied, "You're lucky . . . that is worth sixty points!"

Of course, a Catholic theologian would correct the story just a bit. Strictly speaking, the forty points that came through baptism, the Mass, confession, and good works were also grace. God gave the man the grace to do good deeds, the theologian would say. Yes, the argument goes, works are a part of salvation, but this does not deny grace.

But can good works be smuggled into the message of the gospel under the guise of grace?

Jesus told a parable about two men who went into the temple to pray (Luke 18:9-14). The Pharisee was a religious leader; the publican was regarded as the scum of the earth. The Pharisee "gave thanks to God" that he was not like other men. Then he listed his good works—fasting, tithing, prayer. Note well that he did not take credit for his accomplishments; he realized these had been done by the grace of God.

But the publican knew he was a sinner. He made no effort to list the good he had done. If we say it was because he had done no good deeds we miss the point. The fact is that standing in the presence of God *he knew that anything he would mention would be as dung* (Paul's description in Philippians 3) in the presence of a holy God. Thus seeing his need, he cast himself *entirely* upon the mercy of God. He went home justified; the religious man did not.

The works the Pharisee had done in response to God's grace did not justify him. The publican was justified because he knew that no good deeds could save him.

This parable confirms the words of Isaiah, "All of our righteous deeds are like a filthy garment" (Isa. 64:6). No human merit is ever accepted by God for justification. Just as it is possible to add a billion bananas and never get an orange, so all the human goodness added together can never be transformed into God's righteousness. Only Christ's merit is accepted.

That is why Paul argued that grace and works were antithetical: "But if it is by grace, it is no longer on the basis of works, otherwise grace is no longer grace" (Rom. 11:6).

Life's most important question must be answered with clarity. "By grace you have been saved through faith; and that not of yourselves, it is the gift of God; not as a result of works, that no one should boast" (Eph. 2:8-9).

What is saving faith? First, it involves *knowledge,* the fact of Christ's death for sinners. Second, it means that we *assent* to the truths of salvation; finally, it involves *trust,* the transferring of all of our confidence to Christ alone. Not Christ *and* the church; not Christ *and* baptism; not Christ *and* good deeds. Whether our faith is little or great is not as important as the object of faith. Our faith should be directed to Christ alone.

Bishop Munsey tells a parable of a man who, while walking along, suddenly fell off the edge of a cliff. As he was hurled down he was able to reach out and grab a limb jutting out of the rock. He grasped it and hung there between life and death. Below, he saw the jagged rocks awaiting his fall. Suddenly an angel appeared to him, and the man pleaded for the angel to save him. The angel responded, "Do you believe I can save you?"

The man saw the strong arms of the angel and said, "Yes, I believe you are able to save me."

The angel asked, "Do you believe I will save you?"

The man saw the smile on the angel's face and replied, "Yes, I believe you will save me."

"Then," said the angel, "if you believe that I can save you, and if you believe that I will save you, let go!"

That "letting go" is faith. Christ wants us to rest our full intellectual, emotional, and spiritual weight on him alone. That is saving faith in Christ, who alone is qualified to reconcile us to God. Those who made such a transfer of trust no longer owe God any righteousness.

Augustus Toplady captured the essence of the Good News:

*Not the labors of my hands
Can fulfill thy law's demands;
Could my zeal no respite know,
Could my tears forever flow,
All for sin could not atone;
Thou must save, and thou alone.*

## Notes

1. Reinhold Seeberg, *Text-Book of the History of Doctrine,* trans. Charles Hay (Grand Rapids, Baker, 1964) I, 61.
2. Ibid., 68.
3. Ibid., 78.
4. Louis Berkhof, *The History of Christian Doctrines* (Grand Rapids, Baker, 1937), 208.
5. Seeberg, 129.
6. *The Saint Joseph Baltimore Catechism* (New York: Catholic Book Publishing Co., 1969), 184.
7. Ibid., 206-207.
8. Fulton J. Sheen, *Peace of Soul* (New York: McGraw-Hill, 1949), 208-209.
9. Roland H. Bainton, *Here I Stand—A Life of Martin Luther* (New York: The New American Library, 1950), 41.
10. Ibid., 42.
11. Henry Bettenson, ed., *Documents of the Christian Church* (New York: Oxford University Press, 1963), 263.
12. Benjamin B. Warfield, *The Plan of Salvation* (Grand Rapids: Eerdmans, n.d.), 55-56.
13. Ibid., 68.

# SIX

# Why Can't We Agree about the Lord's Supper?

"Is there anything more sorrowful, more deserving of tears than that [the Lord's Supper] should be used as a subject of strife and division?" Philip Melanchthon asked this question in August 1544. He had good reason to be sorrowful. A few years earlier, Martin Luther and Ulrich Zwingli debated the Lord's Supper at the Marburg Castle in Germany. Flanked by a few friends, Luther and Zwingli sat at opposite ends of a long table surrounded by observers.

Luther reluctantly attended under growing pressure to unify the reform movement in Germany and Switzerland. Prudence required a united front against the growing opposition of the Catholic church. If Luther and Zwingli could agree on the Lord's Supper, theological as well as poilitical unity between the two countries could be achieved.

It was not to be.

Luther held tenaciously to his convictions and even inferred that the Swiss were not brothers in Christ. According to church historian Philip Schaff, after the debate, Zwingli approached Luther with tears and held out a hand of brotherhood, but Luther declined it. The first Protestant council ended unsuccessfully.

Going back to the beginning, we can see how the observance of the Lord's Supper developed in the history of Christian thought. Then we will understand more clearly why Luther and Zwingli differed from the Catholic church and from each other.

## The Lord's Supper in the New Testament

Read the account of the Lord's Supper in the New Testament and you are immediately struck with the simplicity of this special event:

*And while they were eating, Jesus took some bread, and after a blessing, He broke it and gave it to the disciples, and said, "Take, eat; this is My body." And when He had taken a cup and given thanks, He gave it to them, saying, "Drink from it, all of you; for this is My blood of the covenant, which is poured out for many for forgiveness of sins." (Matt. 26:26-28)*

The ceremony seems uncomplicated and clear in its purpose. But Christ did say, "This *is* My body" and "This *is* My blood." So questions inevitably arose about the meaning of these words.

The early church, following the pattern of Christ, had a simple service. Justin Martyr, (ca. 100–165) in his *Apology,* a book written to defend Christianity, wrote that the bishop or church leader began the communion service with a prayer of praise and thanksgiving spoken over the elements. The congregation answered "Amen," and there followed a kiss of brotherly love, which indicated the reconciliation of hearts.

The apostolic fathers rightly began to attach great significance to this act of our Lord. And since Christ instituted this observance after he and the disciples had eaten the Passover feast, it was natural for the early church to commemorate Christ's death after a common meal. The prayer of thanksgiving *(euchristia)* eventually became attached to the supper itself. Later it was changed from a simple prayer of thanksgiving to a prayer of consecration of the bread and wine.

But how were these elements understood? Quotations from the church fathers would indicate that Christ was considered present in the elements. Ignatius of Antioch (ca. 115) said, "The Eucharist is the flesh of our Savior, Jesus Christ, which suffered for our sins, which the Father in his goodness raised from the dead."[1] Basing his conclusion on John 6:54-58, Ignatius spoke of the Lord's Supper as the medicine of immortality. By eating and drinking we become partakers of eternal life.

Justin Martyr said that the elements are not regarded as ordinary bread and wine, "but as our Redeemer, Jesus Christ, was incarnated by the Word of God . . . so [the elements] are both the flesh and blood of that same incarnate Jesus."[2]

By the third century the idea arose that the Lord's Table was a source of spiritual nourishment to those who participated. Tertullian said, "The flesh is refreshed with the body and blood of Christ so that the soul also may be nourished by God."[3]

How shall we summarize the teaching of the Lord's Table during the second and third centuries? Jaroslav Pelikan, in his book *The Christian Tradition,* published by the University of Chicago Press, wrote that no orthodox father of whom we have record declared the presence of the body and blood of Christ in the Eucharist to be only symbolic (though Clement and Origen came close to doing so), nor were there any who specified that the elements were substantially changed (though Ignatius and Justin came close to doing so). Then he adds, "Within the limits of these two extremes was the doctrine of the real presence."[4]

The doctrine of the real presence means that the body and blood of Christ were somehow combined with the elements. When Christ was so remembered, he was there among his people who were participating in redemption. Some saw it as a nourishing of the body; others believed it was symbolic.

Augustine, for example, spoke of the bread and wine as the body and blood of Christ, but at the same time he clearly distinguished between the sign and the thing signified. In other words, he asserted that the substances themselves remained unchanged. To him, eating the flesh of Christ was symbolic. Berkhof wrote, "He stressed the commemorative aspect of the rite and maintained that the wicked, though they may receive the elements, do not partake of the body. He even protested against the superstitious reverence that was paid to the ordinance by many in his day."[5]

Back in the fourth century, the Eucharist became known as the *Mass,* a word whose root meaning is derived from the Latin *missa,* "to dismiss." The word referred to the words spoken by the priest at the end of the feast and later was applied to the entire ritual.

In summary, during the first eight centuries of the church the general consensus was toward a realistic view of the elements: Christ is spiritually present in the bread and wine. To partake is to eat the body and blood of Christ, but not in a literal sense.

## Transubstantiation

In A.D. 818 an abbot of the famous monastery north of Paris at Corbie, named Paschasius Radbertus, published a paper in which he affirmed that the elements were transformed into the actual body and blood of Christ. Though the appearance of the elements do not change, a miracle does take place at the words of the priest—the wine and bread become the literal body and blood of the historical Christ. He affirmed that the outward appearances are but a veil that deceive the senses.

This teaching did not go unchallenged. Theologians such as Rabanus Maurus pointed out that such a belief confuses the sign with that which is signified. In 1050 Berenger of Tours expounded the view that the body and blood of Christ were present not in essence but in power. The substance remained unchanged; faith on the part of the recipient was needed to make the power effectual. The philosopher John Scotus agreed with Augustine that the elements were symbolical, and that they remained unchanged.

The controversy continued more than a hundred years. In the year 1089 a bishop named Humbert said, rather crassly, that "the very body of Christ was truly held in the priest's hand broken and chewed by the teeth of the faithful." Thus the elements were regarded as the very body and blood of the historical Christ. Hildebert of Tours defended this view and is the first to call the change in the elements *transubstantiation*. The Fourth Lateran Council in 1225 ratified this doctrine.

The famous theologian Thomas Aquinas found in Aristotle a philosophical conception to explain how the elements could be changed though their appearance remained unaffected. We know objects by their secondary qualities—such as weight, color, and odor. But the actual *substance* is the inmost essence of a thing and is unknown to us. For example, a ball of wax may change its shape, color, and odor and yet we know it is the same substance; so in the case of the Mass, the secondary qualities remain the same, but the invisible substance is changed. This change of substance takes place at the prayer of consecration, but the secondary qualities remain unaffected. This explains why the elements, if examined in a laboratory, would show no hint of change. But in fact a miracle has taken place—their essence, which is beyond the reach of our senses, has been transformed.

This explanation had the advantage of being incapable of refutation. After all, since the substance of a thing is always beyond the grasp of our senses, no one can disprove the theory. But obviously it could not be proven either. The skeptical among us want to ask how a substance can change without the visible qualities changing along with it. Of course, God is able to do a miracle, but the other miracles in the New Testament could be verified by sight and touch. Why should the transformation of the elements be a special case? One historian said that faith was out, magic was in.

Thomas's doctrines were dogmatized by the Catholic church. In fact, the Council of Trent in 1546 affirmed that the *entire* body and blood of Christ, together with his soul and divinity, are truly present at the Eucharist. Even when one of the elements is divided, the whole Christ is present in each of the parts.

Ideas have consequences. Once the premise was accepted that the elements were literally the body and blood of Christ, other traditions grew around the Mass at various stages of history.

First, the priest was granted extraordinary powers. He had the ability to take ordinary bread and wine and at his command change them into the body and blood of Christ. A statement of this teaching appears in a handbook entitled *The Dignity and Duties of the Priest*:

*With regard to the power of the priests over the real body of Christ, it is of faith that when they pronounce the words of consecration, the incarnate God has obliged Himself to obey and come into their hands under the sacramental appearance of bread and wine. . . . God Himself descends on the altar. . . . He comes whenever they call Him, and as often as they call Him, and places Himself in their hands, even though they should be His enemies. And after having come He remains, entirely at their disposal, and they move Him as they please from one place to another. They may, if they wish, shut Him up in the tabernacle, or expose Him on the altar, or*

*carry Him outside the church; they may, if they choose,
eat His flesh and give Him for the food of others.*[6]

Once consecrated, the elements are the literal body
and blood of Christ in *his entirety.* The Council of Trent
said that the highest form of worship—worship worthy of
God himself—may be rendered to these transformed
elements. The faithful may "render in veneration the
worship of latria, which is due to the true God, to this
holy sacrament."[7]

Since the earthly body of Christ was a sacrifice on the
cross, the idea arose that Christ was now resacrificed in
the Mass. After all, if the elements are literal, the Incarnation takes place again and again. So it seemed reasonable
to assume that he should also be sacrificed again and
again. To quote the Baltimore Catechism: "The Mass
continues the Sacrifice of the Cross. Each time the Mass is
offered, the Sacrifice of Christ is repeated. A new sacrifice
is not offered, but by divine power, one and the same
sacrifice is repeated."[8]

The words, "A new sacrifice is not offered," should not
be interpreted to mean that the Mass is somehow symbolic of the sacrifice of Christ. The Council of Trent
explicitly stated that in the Mass a true and proper pro-
pitiatory sacrifice is offered to God, valid for both the
living and the dead. The sacrifice in the Mass is identical
with the sacrifice of the cross, inasmuch as Jesus Christ is
both a priest and victim. The only difference lies in the
manner of offering, which is bloody upon the cross and
bloodless on the altar. It has been estimated that Christ is
sacrificed as often as two hundred thousand times per
day, worldwide.

Understandably, liturgy developed that would be in
keeping with this exalted view of the elements. The
simple prayer Christ prayed at the first supper evolved
into a detailed ritual. The Mass soon bore little re-
semblance to the Gospel accounts. The pageantry became

so elaborate that Voltaire called it "the grand opera of the poor."

The common people were not allowed to partake of the cup (the blood). After all, they might spill the blood of Christ. Then the notion arose that even the Host (the wafer) should not be eaten unless the participant had not eaten for several hours lest the flesh of Christ be mixed with other foods. This, of course, was contrary to Christ's command to his disciples, "Drink from it, all of you" (Matt. 26:27). And Mark records, "And they all drank from it" (14:23). Notice that in the New Testament the disciples *both* ate the bread and drank the cup. What is more, they did this immediately after eating the Passover meal.

One tradition led to another. The Mass began to be used, not merely for the living, but also for the dead. Since the church's power over the human soul does not end at death, a Mass can be said for the departed. In fact, there are several different kinds of Masses: (1) the *Votive* Mass, made for special occasions of need, such as when facing a decision or crisis; (2) the *Requiem* or funeral Mass on behalf of the dead; (3) the *Nuptial* Mass at marriages and (4) the *Pontifical* Mass, conducted by a bishop or other dignitary. These are available either in low or high Mass format (high Mass is sung and often accompanied by a choir).

By now, even the pretense that these practices are based on the Scriptures has vanished. What remains is an elaborate ritual that is believed to turn common elements into the actual body and blood of Christ. Here Christ is reoffered, grace is received, and God and man meet. It is the high point of Catholic worship.

## Is the Mass a Sacrifice?

Whether or not we agree that the elements are actually transformed, there is an even more important question to be discussed. Must Christ offer himself as a sacrifice again and again? Remember, the Mass is not merely a reenactment of Christ's sufferings; the official Catholic position is that *Christ is repeatedly sacrificed.*

The Roman Catholic church bases its understanding of sacrifice on the Old Testament rituals, where sacrifices were continuously offered. This explains why Catholicism teaches that salvation is a process that is never finished. Even if the past is forgiven, tomorrow is another day. Mass, confession, prayers to Mary—these never settle one's relationship with God forever. Consistency dictates that Christ's sacrifice on the cross is never finished either. He is offered up repeatedly.

However, the New Testament Book of Hebrews explicitly states that Christ's sacrifice was sufficient for God, thus it was offered *once for all.* Four contrasts are made between Christ's sacrifice and those of the Old Testament (Heb. 10:10-14):

1. In the Old Testament many priests offered sacrifices; in fact, they worked in shifts. But now there is only one High Priest who lives forever.

2. Many sacrifices were offered, day after day, whenever sin was committed. But Christ offered "one sacrifice for sins for all time." His work ended the sacrificial system forever.

3. The Old Testament sacrifices could only take care of past sins—which was the reason they had to be reoffered. But of Christ we read, "For by one offering He has perfected for all time those who are sanctified"(v. 14).

4. The former priests were not allowed to sit down while working their shift. But Christ sat down on the right hand of God the Father because his work was finished.

As mentioned, the Catholic church is based upon the Old Testament model of sacrifices and ritual. The priesthood, the perpetual nature of the offerings, the perception that salvation is unfinished—all of this fails to appreciate the radical difference the coming of Christ made.

## The Reformation

As a devout Catholic, Luther originally believed in transubstantiation, and as a priest consecrated the elements. He read all the manuals and was meticulously prepared for the solemn occasion. He took his place at the altar and began to recite the liturgy until he came to the words, "We offer unto thee, the living, the true, the eternal God." At that point he became terror-stricken. Later he recalled, "Who am I that I should lift up mine eyes or raise my hands to the divine Majesty? The angels surround him. At his nod the earth trembles. And shall I, a miserable pygmy say, 'I want this, I ask for that'? For I am but dust and ashes." As Bainton put it, "The terror of the Holy, the horror of the Infinitude, smote him like a new lightning bolt, and only through fearful restraint could he hold himself at the altar to the end."[9]

The official Roman position was that the elements have intrinsic ability regardless of the character of the priest or even the faith of those who partook of them.

Later, as Luther broke with Rome, he stressed that the value of the Lord's Supper was dependent on the faith of the recipient. He also modified his belief in transubstantiation to what is called the real presence or *consubstantiation*. Christ was literally present in the elements, but they were unchanged. Thus he held to literalness without the transformation.

The Reformers rejected the sacrificial theory of the Lord's Supper. But when they formulated their own understanding of this feast, their ways parted. Because the Lord's Supper was central to their worship and service, their convictions were deeply held.

Thus, when Luther and Zwingli met at Marburg, a spirited discussion was inevitable. Previously, Zwingli had written that Christ could not possibly be physically present in the Lord's Supper because his body could exist in only one of three ways, as natural, risen, or mystical. Christ cannot be naturally present in the elements because "the flesh profits nothing" (John 6:63). Nor could the risen body of Christ be present because his words "this is my body" were spoken to the disciples before the resurrection. And Christ could not be mystically present because his mystical body is the church, which is not referred to as delivered unto death. By the process of elimination, Zwingli concluded that the elements were symbolic only.

In reply, Luther had written a pamphlet in which he expounded his view of the real presence of Christ in the sacrament. He held that "each of Christ's natures permeates the other and his humanity participates in the attributes of his divinity." If God is omnipresent, Luther argued, so the body and blood of Christ is omnipresent and possible in the sacrament. He wanted the words of Christ to be taken literally, though he denied there was a change in the substances.

During the debate, no new arguments were advanced, but the exchange did clarify the points of contention.

Luther thundered, "Your basic contentions are these: In the last analysis you wish to prove that a body cannot be at two places at once. . . . I do not question how Christ can be God and man and how the two natures are joined. For God is more powerful than all our ideas, and we must submit to his Word. Prove that Christ's body is not where the Scripture says it is when Christ says 'this is my body.'

"Rational proofs I will not listen to. Corporeal proofs, arguments based on geometrical principles I repudiate absolutely. God is beyond all mathematics, and the words of God are to be revered and carried out in awe. It is God who commands, 'take, eat, this is my body.' I request therefore, valid scriptural proofs to the contrary."

At this point, Luther wrote the words, "This is my body" on the table in chalk and covered it with a velvet cloth.

Zwingli countered, "It is prejudice, a preconception, which keeps Dr. Luther from yielding his point. He refuses to yield until a passage is quoted that proves that the body in the Lord's Supper is figurative.

"Comparison of scriptural passages is always necessary.

Though we have no scriptural passage that says, 'This is the sign of the body,' we still have proof that Christ dismissed the idea of a physical [meal]. In John 6 Christ moves away from the idea of a physical [meal]. From this it follows that Christ did not give himself in the Lord's Supper in a physical sense.

"You yourself have acknowledged that it is the spiritual [meal] that offers solace. And since we are agreed on this major question, I beg you for the love of Christ not to burden anyone with the crime of heresy because of these differences."

Zwingli then demonstrated from Scripture that some statements are symbolic. He argued that Luther was simply refusing to recognize a figure of speech. But at the end of the debate, Luther stoutly maintained his belief in the real presence, or consubstantiation. To deny this doctrine would lead to accepting other heresies.

Zwingli remained unshaken in his memorial view, comparing the sacrament to a wedding ring that seals the marriage union between Christ and the believer. And because of the tenacity of both sides, the division remained, as is evident even today between Lutheran and Reformed churches.[10]

So far we have considered three views of the Lord's Supper: *transubstantiation, consubstantiation,* and the *memorial* view. But there is a fourth. Calvin offered a compromise between the latter two. He held to what is called the *spiritual presence* of Christ in the sacrament. In this sense, it seals and confirms the promise of Christ. The Holy Spirit causes the bread and wine to become our spiritual food. For Calvin, Christ is not literally present, but the elements are more than symbols; they convey spiritual reality.

### Literal or Figurative?

The pivotal question in this discussion hinges on the interpretation of the words of Christ, "This is My body.

This cup is the new covenant in My blood." Should they be interpreted literally or figuratively?

There are several indications in the passage itself that the words are figurative. For example, Jesus said, "This cup is the new covenant in My blood." All scholars, Protestant and Catholic, admit that Christ did not mean that the cup he held in his hand was the New Covenant. The word *cup* was used to refer to the contents inside it. Obviously they did not drink the cup, but its contents. Such symbolism is used in all languages.

More important, Christ called the bread *bread* and the wine *wine* even after he had consecrated it. After he admonished them to eat and drink, he said that he himself would not drink of the fruit of the vine until the kingdom of God comes (Luke 22:18). He was calling what he had just blessed "the fruit of the vine." So Christ did not call the consecrated elements flesh and blood but bread and wine. In the same way, Paul even more explicitly speaks about eating the *bread* and drinking the cup in an unworthy manner. *After the prayer of consecration,* he still called them the bread and the cup. When Christ spoke these words, he was sitting at the table with them in a human body that had as yet not been glorified. Blood was flowing through his veins. In what sense, therefore, could the bread and wine on the table have been his body and blood?

We often show a friend a photograph and say, "Here is my daughter." Christ himself used figurative language more times than I care to recount. He said, "I am the true vine" and again, "I am the door." Symbolism here would be natural and appropriate.

If the Supper is interpreted as symbolic, does this detract from the sacredness of the occasion? I think not. We treat a flag with respect even though it is not a country but merely a representation of it. So the elements are to be handled with reverence because of their profound symbolism.

Often, however, the Catholic church has appealed to
Christ's words, in which he claimed to be the Bread of Life:

*"Truly, truly, I say to you, unless you eat the flesh of the
Son of Man and drink His blood, you have no life in
yourselves. He who eats My flesh and drinks My blood
has eternal life, and I will raise him up on the last day.
For My flesh is true food, and My blood is true drink. He
who eats My flesh and drinks My blood abides in Me,
and I in him." (John 6:53-56)*

Since cannibalism is inconsistent with the general
teaching of Scripture, it is unlikely that Christ intended
these words literally. What is more, the Old Testament
explicitly forbids drinking blood (Lev. 17:10). The first
church council in Jerusalem ratified this prohibition (Acts
15:29).

The clue to Christ's meaning is found in the Passover of
the Old Testament where the Jews ate the lamb and drank
the Passover wine. Christ, Paul says, is now our Passover.
He is the fulfillment of this feast. Therefore, a person's
relationship with him is what gives life. But are we to
literally eat his flesh and drink his blood? If so, the Jews to
whom Christ spoke would not have had an opportunity to
receive eternal life since they were not able to meet this
requirement. Christ explained what he meant:

*"As the living Father sent Me, and I live because of the
Father, so he who eats Me, he also shall live because of
Me. This is the bread which came down out of heaven;
not as the fathers ate, and died; he who eats this bread
shall live forever." (John 6:57-58)*

How shall we eat Christ? Just as he lived by his relationship to his Father, so we are to live by him. Christ is food
for the soul; he is bread and water to those who are spiritually destitute. Lest we should misunderstand him, a para-

graph later Christ said, "It is the Spirit who gives life; the flesh profits nothing" (v. 63).

The Lord's Supper should be primarily a time of reflection and worship. Though we must steadfastly reject any misleading traditions, we must remember our Lord's death in the way he designated. In many of our Protestant churches the Lord's Supper must be restored to its place of prominence. We must never lose the wonder and the mystery of this feast in a day of short sermons and pop religion.

The privilege of participation should never be taken for granted. We can imagine the elation in Wittenberg on Christmas Day 1521, when two thousand people assembled in the Castle Church, and Carlstadt, an associate of Luther, distributed both bread and wine to the congregation. A privilege denied to believers for hundreds of years was restored. The Reformers called this the priesthood of the believer.

If Melanchthon were alive today, he might not weep because of controversies that surround the Lord's Supper, but he might well sorrow because of our indifference to its meaning and importance. This, too, is deserving of tears.

### Notes

1. Reinhold Seeberg, *Textbook of the History of Christian Doctrines*, trans. Charles E. Hay (Grand Rapids: Baker, 1964), 1:68.
2. Ludwig Ott, *Fundamentals of Catholic Dogma*, trans. Patrick Lynch (St. Louis: B. Herder Book Co., 1957), 376.
3. Ibid., 377.
4. Jaroslav Pelikan, *The Christian Tradition* (Chicago: University of Chicago Press), 167.
5. Louis Berkhof, *The History of Christian Doctrines* (Grand Rapids: Baker, 1937), 252.
6. Alphonse de Liguori, *The Dignity and Duty of the Priest* (Milwaukee, Wis.: Our Blessed Lady of Victory Mission, 1927).
7. Philip Schaff, *The Creeds of Christendom* (Grand Rapids: Baker, 1983), 2:131.

8. *The New Saint Joseph Baltimore Catechism* (New York: Catholic Publishing House, 1962), 171.
9. Roland H. Bainton, *Here I Stand: A Life of Martin Luther* (New York: The New York American Library, 1950), 30.
10. Donald J. Ziegler, ed., *Great Debates of the Reformation* (New York: Random House, 1969), 71-107.

# Why Can't We Agree about Baptism?

You have probably heard the story about the Baptist and Presbyterian having a discussion about the proper form of baptism. "If a person is baptized up to his neck, is he really baptized?" the Presbyterian asked.

"No, of course not," the Baptist replied.

"If he is baptized up to his forehead, is that baptism?"

"No," the Baptist said emphatically.

"Well," said the Presbyterian, "that proves that it's the water on the head that really makes the difference!"

Water baptism has been a source of controversy in Christendom since the early beginnings of the church. In the Book of Acts it is closely associated with the conversion experience. "Repent, and let each of you be baptized in the name of Jesus Christ for the forgiveness of your sins; and you shall receive the gift of the Holy Spirit" (Acts 2:38). Texts such as this one have spawned disagreements which are still debated today.

Three questions are often asked: (1) Should water baptism be limited to adults who have personally believed on Christ or should infants be included? (2) Is baptism a means of grace whereby a person is regenerated? (3) Less important, what is the mode of baptism—that is, should we immerse, sprinkle, or pour water on the head?

## The Rise of Infant Baptism

Perhaps the best defense of infant baptism that has ever been written is Geoffery Bromiley's book *Children of Promise.* He begins with the statement, "The chief difficulty in relation to the New Testament is that it does not give us the plain and direct evidence for or against infant baptism which most people desire and which many think they find in it."[1]

Bromiley admitted what all paedobaptists (those who believe in the baptism of infants) have acknowledged, namely, that there is no evidence that infants were baptized in the churches of the New Testament. Some have suggested that, in the household baptisms in the Book of Acts, infants may have been included, but this is conjecture. In fact, the evidence points in the opposite direction, since the text in some cases explicitly states that baptism was given to those who responded to the message. For example, in the case of the Philippian jailer, we read, "And they spoke the word of the Lord to him together with all who were in his house" (Acts 16:32). This explains why his household could be baptized—they all were old enough to hear the Word. Infant baptism, as we shall see, rests on other theological premises.

In the New Testament, baptism followed immediately after personal faith in Christ was exercised. As far as we can tell, there were no unbaptized believers in the early church. All believers were baptized as a witness to their faith.

Where then did infant baptism arise? We might expect to find references to it in the writings of the church fathers, that is, those who knew the apostles. Not so. For example, Irenaeus, who was acquainted with Polycarp, a disciple of the Apostle John, wrote a five-volume treatise on theology yet made no reference to infant baptism.

In the Epistle of Barnabas (ca. 120-130), a brief chapter is devoted to baptism, but only the baptism of believers. "We go down into the water full of sins and foulness, and we come up bearing fruit in our hearts, fear and hope in Jesus in the Spirit."[2] Even more telling is the fact that in the *Didache,* an early handbook on Christian ministry (ca. 100-110), there is detailed instruction on the moral conduct of the one who is baptized. It explains that running water should be used; if this is not available then standing water. If there is not enough water available for immersion, then water may be poured on the head three times in the name of the Father, the Son, and the Holy Spirit. But there is no mention of infant baptism.

Where do we find the first references to infant baptism? With the rise of sacramentalism (discussed in a previous chapter), baptism and Communion were both believed to be means of grace given to the Church. If so, it seemed logical to administer them to infants as well as adults. Our first explicit reference to infant baptism comes from Tertullian, a leader in the church in North Africa (ca. 200). Tertullian argued against the practice, insisting that children should come for baptism when they were grown up so they would understand what they are doing. "Therefore, according to everyone's condition and disposition, and also his age, the delaying of baptism is more profitable, especially in the case of little children."[3] His objection shows that by the year 200 it was already practiced in some churches.

The second reference to infant baptism comes from the writings of Origen, who was born into a Christian family in Alexandria, Egypt. He enjoyed fame as a teacher, though eventually he was forced to move to Palestine because of the antagonism of the bishop of Alexandria. In a commentary on the Book of Luke, he wrote that infants are baptized "that the pollution of our birth be taken away." He repeated essentially the same statement in a commentary on Romans.

Scholars differ as to how much weight should be given to these passages. Although Origen wrote in Greek, these texts exist only in a Latin translation made by one named

Rufinus, who lived at a later period and who was notorious for adding his own opinions to his translations. Some think he added these references to infant baptism to harmonize Origen's teaching with the beliefs of the Latin church of his day. If the statements of Origen are authentic, however, they do represent an important witness to both the fact of infant baptism and its rationale in the church by the year 240.

The third reference is found in the writings of Cyprian, also from North Africa. In about 251, he asked the delegates at a church council whether they felt that baptism should be delayed until the eighth day. He records that the council, composed of sixty-six bishops, said that baptism should not be delayed "lest in doing so we expose the soul of the child to the risk of eternal perdition." Here we have an explicit reference that links the baptism of infants with spiritual regeneration. In a later document, Cyprian also mentioned that infants should be given Communion, too. If, indeed, grace is communicated through the sacraments, infants should not be denied this blessing.

Augustine is our fourth witness from North Africa who advocated infant baptism. As we have learned, he had a great impact on the thinking of the Christian church. He taught that infant baptism went back to apostolic times, though he does not cite by name anyone who taught it earlier than Cyprian. Consistent with the theology of the area, he also gives apostolic authority to the practice of infant Communion. Both of the sacraments are necessary for salvation, therefore, both should be administered for infants. "If then, as so many divine testimonies agree, neither salvation nor eternal life is to hoped for by any, without baptism and the body and blood of our Lord, it is in vain promised to infants without them."[4]

Churches that believed in sacramentalism, then, administered both ordinances to infants. Jewett commented, "Nor did it ever occur to anyone in the ancient church to question the right of infants to the Eucharist once the right to embrace them in the church had been established." The theory that infants are to be baptized but not given communion, says Jewett, "rests on medieval dogmatic developments in the Western church that had nothing to do with an evangelical view of the sacraments."[5]

With the development of infant baptism, the idea of having parents to sponsor the child arose. Tertullian, who spoke against infant baptism, referred to these sponsors as being in danger of making rash promises when they said that the child would be a Christian in later life. "Who can know if this will happen?" he asked.

The practice of infant baptism, then, arose in North Africa sometime in the latter part of the second century, largely due to the belief that forgiveness of sins came through the sacraments. In keeping with this sacramentalism, Communion was given to infants as well.

## The Significance of Infant Baptism in Medieval Times

Anyone familiar with the history of Christianity knows that the early church experienced bitter opposition from the Roman Empire. Wave after wave of persecution came to believers. It was not that the Romans were intolerant of other religions—indeed, one could worship whatever god he liked. It was the exclusivism of Christianity that irritated the Roman emperors. Christians were so narrow-minded they would not say, "Caesar is Lord!"

The emperor Diocletian ruled for twenty years. Before he died, he turned against Christians, purging them from the empire. In A.D. 305, he abdicated the throne and bequeathed it to Galerius, who was even more vehement against the Christians. On his deathbed in 311, Galerius realized that even the pagans were sickened by the bloody persecution. Knowing that the general populace was turning against him, he issued the edict of toleration, which, for the most part, gave the Christians reprieve. Upon his death, a power struggle broke out and Constantine advanced across the Alps to dislodge the Roman ruler Maxentius (who hoped to follow Galerius) and capture Rome. When Constantine met his rival at the Mivian bridge just outside of Rome, he turned for help to the Christian God. In a dream he saw a cross in the sky and the words, "In this sign conquer." When he achieved military success on October 28, A.D. 312, he looked upon his victory as proof of the truth of the Christian religion. Whether or not his conversion was genuine, he did give Christians freedom and eventually Christianity became the official religion of the empire.

What does all of this have to do with baptism? With Constantine in power, Christianity was no longer a sect within the empire but was to become synonymous with the empire. One would now be a Christian simply by being born into the empire, not necessarily by having personal faith in Christ. *Infant baptism became the link by which the church and the state were united.*

Although infant baptism began for theological reasons, namely, the belief that the ritual washed away the pollution of sins, it now became a political asset. Every child christened was both a Christian and a member of the Roman empire. Since infants could become citizens of the empire without any decision on their part, so too they could become Christians. Infant baptism thus became an almost universal practice in a matter of decades.

Augustine gave credence to the belief that the church and state should be united by affirming (1) the right of the church to use the state in the enforcement of Christianity. Thus "heretics" could be killed and dissenters massacred; and (2) infant baptism should be required.

Infant baptism played a crucial role in the marriage of church and state. This is why the Anabaptists (those who were rebaptized as adults) were persecuted so severely. The dispute was not merely theological but political. During the days of Charlemagne (crowned in the year A.D.

800), those who were rebaptized after personally believing in Christ were put to death. The fear was that if the church was considered only a group within society rather than coextensive with society, the whole unity of the church and state would be fragmented. Infant baptism was the "glue" that united church and state.

The famous Swiss theologian Karl Barth admitted that the real motivation behind infant baptism was *Constantinianism*, that is, the unity of church and state. Speaking about the Reformers who held to infant baptism, he commented, "Men at the time would not renounce, for love or money, the existence of the Evangelical church in the form of the Constantinian *corpus Christianum*. When the church breaks with infant baptism, People's church in the sense of a state church or a mass church is finished." He went on to say that even Luther confessed that there would not be too many baptized people if a man, instead of being *brought* to baptism, had to *come* to it. Barth pointed out that the Bible teaches that the Christian church is a minority; when everyone is included in it, the result is sickness not health. He concludes by saying that "it is high time to announce that an urgent quest after a better form of our baptismal practice is long overdue."[6]

## The Reformers: Zwingli

Initially Zwingli, the famous preacher of Zurich, had serious doubts about infant baptism. He confessed, "Nothing grieves me more than that at the present I have to baptize children for I know it ought not to be done."[7] He realized that a thorough renewal of the church would mean stopping the practice. Again he said, "I leave baptism untouched, I call it neither right or wrong; if we were to baptize as Christ instituted it, then we would not baptize any person until he has reached the years of discretion; for I find it nowhere written that infant baptism is to be practiced."[8]

But later Zwingli changed his mind. To understand why,

we must refresh our memories about the Anabaptist
movement that spread throughout Europe during the
Reformation.

The word *Anabaptist* applies to those who had been
baptized as infants but who where rebaptized when they
personally came to faith in Christ. The first Anabaptists
were the Donatists of the fourth century who refused to
believe that a baptism that embraced everyone simply
because of an accident of birth could be valid. They
believed that the church should be distinct from society
and not coextensive with it. But as we learned, when the
state became united with the church, the church used the
power of the state to enforce religion. Many Donatists
were killed simply because they held to believer's baptism.

Though Donatism (named after their leader Donatus)
was suppressed, its vision of a church comprised of baptized believers never died out. When these beliefs
emerged centuries later, action was taken against "heretics" who wanted to overturn the practice of infant baptism. There are numerous records of those who protested
against the official church that embraced everyone. These
dissenters wanted to return to the New Testament pattern
where the church was comprised of baptized believers.
They believed that the church is to be kept pure by
complete devotion to Christ and by the exercise of church
discipline. Their conduct was so exemplary that Zwingli
said of them, "At first contact, their conduct appears
irreproachable, pious, unassuming, attractive. Even those
who are inclined to be critical will say that their lives are
excellent."[9]

These Christians could not accept the notion that an
infant could be "christened," that is, made a Christian by
participating in a ritual. They called infant baptism nothing
more than a "dipping in a Romish bath." To them holy
living was proof of regeneration. A Catholic observed in
them "no lying, deception, swearing, strife, harsh language,
no intemperate eating and drinking, no outward personal

display, but rather humility, patience, uprightness, meekness, honesty, temperance, straightforwardness in such measure that one would suppose that they had the Holy Spirit of God."[10]

But the official church, steeped in Constantinianism, used the power of the state to kill the "heretics." And the Reformers themselves became fanatical in their opposition to the Anabaptists when these dissenters insisted on making a clean break with the church of the empire. On the point of infant baptism, Luther and Zwingli sided with the Roman church. Zwingli, for example, saw that if he were to stand with the Anabaptists, he would incur the displeasure of the state. He said, "If, however, I were to terminate the practice, then I fear I would lose my prebend"[11] (a stipend he received for preaching). But more important, he saw the Anabaptists as disrupting the social order.

So he turned against them saying that, although it was necessary to condemn infant baptism at first, times had now changed; he confessed to being misled. He also restudied the Scriptures and concluded that infant baptism could be justified on theological grounds (we will consider these arguments later in this chapter).

The city council of Zurich told him that by preaching against infant baptism, "the holy church, the ancient fathers, the Councils, the pope, the cardinals, and bishops, etc., will be made to look ridiculous, will be disdained and eliminated."[12] What is more, the council went on to say that if baptism were limited to believers, there would be "disobedience to the magistracy, disunity, heresy, and the weakening and diminution of the Christian faith."

So it was that on January 17, 1525, the city council of Zurich notified the public that all parents *had* to have their children baptized or be banished. Four years later, the edict of Speier decreed, "Every Anabaptist or rebaptized person, of either sex, is to be put to death, by fire or by sword, or by some other means."[13] Children were baptized against their parent's wishes. Those who stood by their convictions and refused to submit to the council were drowned or executed. Zwingli sarcastically remarked about the Anabaptist Felix Manz, "If he wishes to go under the water, then let him go under." Thus Manz was forcibly drowned in the deep, cold waters of the Limmat River just a few hundred yards from Zwingli's church. Many died saying that Zwingli had betrayed them. He had sold his soul to a false Christendom that refused to distinguish between the true church and society.

It's easy to be critical of Zwingli, since for us the separation of church and state is taken for granted. But he lived in a day when one purpose of the state was to be sure that the will of God was done in the lives of those who lived within its borders. Unfortunately, persecution caused some of the Anabaptists to become fanatics. Such radicals gave the Anabaptist movement a bad name, which only gave cause for more persecution. Yet the massacre of the Anabaptists is surely one of the darkest pages in church history.

## The Reformers: Luther

And what about Luther and infant baptism? He waffled on the matter saying, "There is not sufficient evidence from Scripture that one might justify the introduction of infant baptism at the time of the early Christians after the apostolic period . . . but so much is evident that no one may venture with good conscience to reject or abandon infant baptism, which for so long time has been practiced."[14]

Luther also gave his approval to the extermination of the Anabaptists. He refused to allow that the true church was to be a group separate from society at large. His friend Melanchthon said of the Anabaptists, "Now let every devout man consider what disruption would ensue if there should develop among us two categories, the baptized and the unbaptized!"[15] He feared that the church would actually be distinct from the world. The Anabaptists believed that infant baptism was the cornerstone of the papal order; until it was removed there could be no Christian congregation.

So Luther did not give up the practice of infant baptism. When the Zwickau prophets pressed for more radical reforms, including the baptism of believers, Luther became adamant against all Anabaptists, insisting that they were instigated by the devil. He reacted strongly against radicals such as Muentzer, who believed that he and his followers could establish the New Jerusalem on earth. Caught in the middle on the topic of infant baptism, Luther talked both ways. He wanted to hold to two doctrines that were in conflict, namely justification by faith and the belief that infants were regenerated by baptism. In his commentary on Galatians, he even suggested that an infant can hear and believe the gospel; in fact, it is easier for a child to believe than an adult because the child is more receptive. In a sermon he suggested that if anyone does not think that baptized infants do not believe, he should cease the practice "so that we no more mock and blaspheme the most blessed majesty of God with such baseless tomfoolery and jugglery."

We must understand Luther's dilemma. He was opposed to the Roman Catholic view that the sacraments had value in taking away sin regardless of whether the participant had faith. Luther stressed that it was faith that saved the soul. So, the only way for the baptism of an infant to have validity was for the child to believe.

But elsewhere he contradicted the idea that faith must be present for baptism to have value. He wrote, in what Verduin says must have been one of his off days:

*How can baptism be more grievously reviled and disgraced than when we say that baptism given to an unbelieving man is not good and genuine baptism! . . . What, baptism rendered ineffective because I do not*

*believe? ... What more blasphemous and offensive
doctrine could the devil himself invent and preach? And
yet the Anabaptists ... are full up to their ears with this
teaching. I put forth the following: Here is a Jew that
accepts baptism, as happens often enough, but does not
believe, would you then say that this was not real baptism, because he does not believe? That would be to
think as a fool thinks not only, but to blaspheme and
disgrace God moreover.*[16]

Today Lutheran churches teach that infants must be
baptized to be regenerated. The liturgy of baptism reads:
"We are born children of fallen humanity; in the waters of
baptism we are reborn children of God and inheritors of
eternal life." Some Lutherans baptize infants who are not
expected to live, believing that this act secures eternal
salvation.

But though the infant becomes a child of God by baptism, the paedobaptists had a problem. Some children did
not grow up to embrace the faith but were reprobates. To
face this dilemma, confirmation was instituted so that a
child would confirm the decision his parents made.
Jewett points out that the necessity of this practice can
mean only one of two things: either the miracle of the
new birth effected through infant baptism is canceled
when the child becomes of age or else confirmation is a
tacit admission that the child was in fact not regenerated
in the first place.

## The Reformers: Calvin

And what about Calvin? He, like Zwingli, found an analogi-
cal relationship between the Old Testament sign of circumcision and the New Testament sign of baptism. The rite of
circumcision proves that God's blessings are given to the
children as well as to their parents. Since the covenant
does not change, why should infants be excluded from

this blessing? He admitted that the Scriptures nowhere record the baptism of an infant, but this, said Calvin, is really no different than the fact that it does not record that a woman took Communion. He scorned the suggestion that the early church did not baptize infants. He can think of "no author, however ancient, who does not regard its origin in the apostolic age as a certainty."

Like Luther, Calvin struggled with the problem of how baptism can be of benefit to an infant who cannot believe. He said that God may have already previously regenerated those infants who are to be saved. Critics have pointed out that if this were true then infants would not be born "in Adam" but "in Christ." This conclusion was not widely accepted.

Calvin has a more plausible suggestion. Baptism does not effect the regeneration of infants but means only that the "seeds of repentance lie in infants by the secret working of the Spirit." They are baptized into future faith and repentance. This does not mean that unbaptized infants should be consigned to eternal death if they die in infancy. Baptism does not effect regeneration but only means that "the seeds of repentance" are present.

Calvin also has an argument for those who say that if infants are baptized they should also be given Communion. He said that water, the sign of the new birth, is proper for infants, but not solid substances. Also, self-examination is specifically required for Communion but not for baptism.

## A Closer Look

At the beginning of this chapter, a book written by Geoffrey Bromiley, *Children of Promise,* in defense of infant baptism, was mentioned. The book turns on the premise, suggested by Calvin, that infant baptism is a sign of the New Covenant just as circumcision was the sign of the Old Covenant. Paul wrote:

*And in Him you were also circumcised with a circumci-*
*sion made without hands, in the removal of the body of*
*the flesh by the circumcision of Christ; having been*
*buried with Him in baptism, in which you were also*
*raised up with Him through faith in the working of God,*
*who raised Him from the dead. (Col. 2:11-12)*

Baptism, Bromiley wrote, is not a sign to those present
at the ritual but a sign to the name and act of God into
which we are caught up in faith. It declares "not what I
do, but what God has done." This explains why it can be
administered to those who have not yet believed. It is not
a sign of their faith but rather a sign of what God has done
(or will do for the recipient).

Bromiley saw baptism as a sign that God has elected the
infant, a view labeled "presumptive election" by those of
the Reformed church who embraced it in Switzerland.
The problem, however, is that some who are presumed to
be elect do not believe when they come of age. Many die
as apostates. Critics are quick to point out that "presumptive election" is indeed too presumptive! Is it not rash to
give the sign of election before we know whether in fact
the child is elect? Why not wait until the child is old
enough to give proof of his election by faith and good
works?

Bromiley answers this objection in two ways:
(1) Although the entire nation of Israel was elected by
God, not all individual Israelites were saved. To put it
differently, all the males were circumcised, but not all
were saved. Just so, all children can be baptized even
though not all will be saved. (2) Even those who practice
believer's baptism run the risk of baptizing those who
turn out to be apostate. Therefore the sign of water can
never be directly equated with election to eternal life.

What benefits come to the children through baptism if
their salvation is not thereby guaranteed? Bromiley admitted they are neither saved by baptism nor is this a guaran-

tee that they will be. They come under the divine promises and share in a corporate election. They grow up
under the "sphere of the divine calling." Baptism is the
outward sign of the grace an infant will receive if he
grows up and believes.

But there is more. Though Bromiley said that infant
baptism does not effect regeneration (here he agreed
with Calvin against Luther), near the end of the book he
said there is a connection between infant baptism and
infant salvation. Since all children are born under the
condemnation of Adam's sin, God must make special
provision for them if they are to be saved. What Bromiley
wanted to suggest was that baptism is the instrument by
which children of believers "enter into the vicarious
reconciliation of the Son according to the election of the
Father." He also agreed with Luther that since faith is a gift
of God, infants can receive faith even when "there is no
normal consciousness of it."

What about infants who are not baptized? Bromiley did
not speculate but hoped that they too shall be saved. But
here, the reader of Bromiley's book reaches an impasse. If
all those who die in infancy are saved, then baptism is not
the means of salvation after all. On the other hand, if only
baptized infants are saved at death, then, contrary to the
assertions Bromiley makes in the first chapters of his
book, baptism is the means of regeneration. The question
is unresolved: does baptism regenerate infants or does it
not?

What shall we make of these arguments? First of all,
those who teach believer's baptism are quick to point out
that Bromiley's parallel between circumcision and baptism
fails because the New Covenant differs significantly from
the Old. It is true that circumcision was routinely administered in the Old Testament, whether or not faith was
present. It was a sign of the blessings of the covenant that
a child could fully receive only when he grew up and had
personal faith.

Under the New Covenant, baptism plays a different role. Only the *spiritual* seed of Abraham receive the sign of baptism. That is, the sign is limited to those who have saving faith. An infant is not yet a member of this spiritual remnant. Baptism is a sign, not of foreseen faith, but of *faith that is already present.* The Reformers themselves knew this; that is why they either took the position that infants could believe, or held to the equally implausible view that the parents or guardian could believe for them.

Circumcision was a sign of earthly, temporal blessings that God gave to the offspring of Abraham. This sign also pointed to ultimate spiritual benefits to those who would believe. In contrast, in the church, one's genealogical record does not guarantee any special blessings. That is why baptism is limited to those who believe and are therefore inheritors of eternal life.

Second, when Bromiley said that infant salvation and infant baptism are connected, he seemed to agree tacitly with Luther that infants are regenerated by baptism. This is why he affirms that infants can believe. This contradicts his earlier assertions that baptism does not regenerate an infant. On the one hand, he argued that baptism is only a sign of future salvation. On the other, he wanted to affirm that baptism regenerates because infants have faith.

Karl Barth said, "There is no getting around that fact, in every attempt, unavoidable as it may be, to think through the relationship between *baptism* and *faith* for a given doctrine of infant baptism, that one shall run into the most unhappy dead-end street, since in this question, one obscurity and perplexity conjures up another; one follows another and that by necessity."[17]

### Controversy in England

The famous preacher Charles Haddon Spurgeon began a storm of controversy when on June 5, 1864, he preached a message against infant baptism from Mark 16:15-16.

Since he so openly criticized the Church of England, he thought it would destroy the ministry of his printed sermons. Just the opposite occurred. He sold more than a quarter of a million copies of this message!

Spurgeon quoted from the Catechism of the Church of England, proving that the church teaches that it is through infant baptism the infant is made a member of Christ, a child of God, and an inheritor of the kingdom of heaven. He quoted from the liturgy of the ceremony itself to further prove that the church did indeed teach that children are regenerated though baptism.

Spurgeon pointed out that no outward ceremony can save anyone. This can be easily proven by the facts: thousands who were baptized as infants have lived wanton, godless lives, proving that they were never children of God. Nor does the Bible teach that someone else can have faith for another; parents cannot believe for their children. To make matters worse, many parents are not even regenerate themselves. So Spurgeon wrote, "Unregenerate sinners promising for a poor babe that he shall keep all God's holy commandments, which they themselves wantonly break every day! How long can the long-suffering of God endure this?"[18]

Lest one should say that the abuse of the practice is no argument against it, Spurgeon would say that the practice itself is an abuse. It rests salvation on the wrong footing, "for of all the lies which have dragged millions down to hell, I look at this as being the most atrocious—that in a Protestant church there should be those who swear that baptism saves the soul."[19] He urged those who may be resting their salvation on this rite to "shake off this venomous faith into the fire as Paul did the viper which fastened to his hand."

Critics responded by reminding Spurgeon that babies were brought to Christ that he might bless them. So Spurgeon preached another sermon proving there is a big difference between bringing children to Christ and bringing them to the font. "See that you read the Word [about blessing the children] as it is written, and you will find no water in it, but Jesus only. Are the water and Christ the same thing? Nay, here is a wide difference, as wide as between Rome and Jerusalem . . . between false doctrine and the gospel of our Lord Jesus Christ."[20]

As far as I know, Spurgeon believed that all infants who die go to heaven. But this is so, not because they are born innocent or because baptism washes away their sins, but because God mercifully laid their sins on Christ. At any rate, the salvation of all infants is in the hands of God, not in the hands of men who administer a ritual.

### Does Baptism Save Anyone?

Does the Bible make baptism necessary for salvation? Some say that adults who have believed are not yet saved until they are also baptized. The Church of Christ, for example, teaches that God works though this ritual to dispense his salvation and grace. Three primary passages of Scripture are used to teach this doctrine. The first is Christ's words to Nicodemus: "Truly, Truly, I say to you, unless one is born of water and the Spirit, he cannot enter into the kingdom of God" (John 3:5).

What did Christ mean? A fundamental rule of interpretation is that we put ourselves into the shoes of the person to whom the words are spoken, in this case Nicodemus. Would he have interpreted the word *water* to refer to baptism? Given his Jewish background, that is indeed unlikely. As a student of the Old Testament, he would probably think of Ezekiel 36:25: "Then I will sprinkle clean water on you, and you will be clean; I will cleanse you from all your filthiness and from all your idols." Here water refers to the Holy Spirit as an agent of cleansing, as the next verse shows. "Moreover, I will give you a new heart and put a new spirit within you."

Greek students have pointed out that Christ may be

using a play on words. The Greek word *pneuma* (translated "spirit") is actually the word for "wind." It can be translated by either "spirit" or "wind," depending on the context. So what Christ might be saying is, "Except a man be born of water and wind, he cannot enter the kingdom of God." A few verses later Christ, using the same word says, "The wind blows where it wills." Both of the natural forces of water and wind are emblems of the Holy Spirit.

At any rate, water is often a picture of the work of the Holy Spirit (as in the passage quoted above). It is unthinkable that Christ should add the requirement of baptism for entrance into the kingdom of heaven when speaking to Nicodemus but mention it nowhere else. If baptism is necessary for salvation, this should have been stated clearly elsewhere. But dozens of times, faith alone is mentioned as the one requirement. Indeed, in the same chapter, *belief* is mentioned as the sole ground of salvation (3:36)

The next passage is Acts 2:38, where Peter said on the Day of Pentecost, "Repent, and let each of you be baptized in the name of Jesus Christ for the forgiveness of your sins; and you shall receive the gift of the Holy Spirit."

The mention of both repentance and baptism does not mean that both are necessary for the forgiveness of sins. I may say, "Take your keys and coat and start the car." That does not mean that taking one's coat is necessary for starting the car even though it is stated along with taking the keys. Repentance, but not baptism, is necessary for the forgiveness of sins.

The Greek grammar confirms this interpretation. The phrase "and be baptized every one of you for the forgiveness of sins" is actually a parenthesis. The command to repent is plural, "ye repent," and so is the phrase "for the forgiveness of your [plural] sins." This means that the command to repent agrees grammatically with the forgiveness of sins. The command to be baptized is singular, "every one of you be baptized," which sets it off from the rest of the sentence. "Repent . . . for the forgiveness of your sins" is the central point. Note that in Acts 10:43, Peter mentioned faith as the only requirement to receive the forgiveness of sins.

The third passage is in 1 Peter 3:21 where Peter wrote, "Corresponding to that, baptism now saves you." But this phrase must be interpreted in light of the context. Baptism is said to save us, just as water saved Noah. How did water save Noah? The water did not save him at all; it was an instrument of judgment. The ark actually saved him by bringing him through the water. This ark was built and entered by faith.

Peter went on to explain that water does not save us either. Baptism saves, he said, but it is not the physical act of washing that does it, "not the removal of dirt from the flesh, but an appeal to God for a good conscience—through the resurrection of Jesus Christ." Water did not save Noah, nor do the waters of baptism save us. What saves? The appeal of a good conscience before God. That word *appeal* can be translated "answer." The people at that time were required to make a statement of faith before baptism. The faith that they testify of is that which saves.

But wait a moment. We know that God grants the gift of salvation to those who believe. How can the statement of faith given at baptism save anyone? Is not such a testimony a result of saving faith rather than the *act* of saving faith? A closer look at the text suggests that what Peter had in mind was that the willingness to confess Christ in baptism *saves one from a guilty conscience.* Note his preceding admonition to "keep a good conscience" (v. 16). The context is one of being willing to suffer for Christ, regardless of the cost. Baptism is a public affirmation of identification with Christ; it saves one from the temptation to be silent about one's faith. It is, Peter said, "an appeal to God for a good conscience."

To summarize the parallel, water didn't save Noah, but

he was brought safely through it because of his faith in God. Nor does water save the person who is baptized; but he also is brought safely through it—it is a picture of death and judgment. He is dipped into it and then back out to symbolize death to his old life and resurrection to the new life. Though persecution may come, he has a clear conscience before God.

If anyone should think that baptism is necessary for salvation from sin, let him contemplate Paul's words to the church at Corinth, where he listed all the people he could remember baptizing—only Crispus and Gaius and the household of Stephanas, then he added, "For Christ sent me not to baptize, but to preach the gospel" (1 Cor. 1:17). If baptism were necessary for salvation, Paul would have made sure that all who believed were baptized. But he distinguished that gospel from the act of baptism.

If baptism were necessary for salvation, the thief on the cross could not have been saved, for he was not baptized after he believed on Christ. Yet he had the assurance from the Master himself, "Truly I say to you, today you shall be with Me in Paradise" (Luke 23:43).

The ordinances in the New Testament are like a wedding ring. It is possible to be married and not have a wedding ring; also, it is possible to wear a wedding ring and not be married. Though baptism receives high priority in the New Testament, it is never considered the means of salvation.

## The Mode of Baptism

What should the *mode* of baptism be? There can be little doubt that the New Testament seems to teach that believers were actually immersed, that is, put under the water and brought up again. Whether it is John the Baptist baptizing in the Jordan, or Philip baptizing the Ethiopian eunuch, the text tells us that they went down into the water and then came up out of the water. This would best depict Paul's description of the baptism of the Spirit as death, burial, and resurrection (Romans 6:1-4).

In the catacombs of Rome there are pictures that show water being poured upon a person's head in the act of baptism. As mentioned, the *Didache*, a manual on church polity that dates back to the second century, taught that if one could not be baptized in running water (such as a river), water should be poured on the head. Obviously, it takes a considerable body of water to immerse an adult, so immersion may not always have been feasible. Pouring water over the head would be sometimes (perhaps often) necessary. Some segments of the church have practiced the sprinkling of water on the head, perhaps to circumvent some of the inconveniences of becoming wet from head to toe.

Whatever mode is agreed upon is, however, secondary to the earlier questions about infant baptism and whether baptism is actually the communication of grace. In these matters the clarity of the gospel message is directly affected.

Unfortunately, there is little hope that Christendom will ever be united on this important ordinance. The basic question again is whether salvation is received by faith alone or whether the sacraments are a part of the conversion experience.

### Notes

1. Geoffery Bromiley, *Children of Promise* (Grand Rapids, Eerdmans, 1979), 1.
2. Paul K. Jewett, *Infant Baptist and the Covenant of Grace* (Grand Rapids, Eerdmans, 1978), 40.
3. Ibid., 20.
4. Ibid., 17-18.
5. Ibid., 42.
6. Ibid., 111.
7. Leonard Verdium, *The Reformers and Their Stepchildren* (Grand Rapids, Eerdmans, 1964), 198.

8. Ibid., 199.
9. Roland H. Bainton, *The Reformation of the Sixteenth Century* (Boston: Beacon Press, 1952), 97.
10. Ibid.
11. Verdium, 199.
12. Ibid., 201.
13. Ibid.
14. Ibid., 204.
15. Ibid., 209.
16. Ibid., 201.
17. Ibid., 185.
18. Charles H. Spurgeon, "Baptismal Regeneration," in *Sermons* (New York: Funk and Wagnalls, n.d.), 8:23.
19. Ibid.
20. Spurgeon, "Children Brought to Christ, Not to the Font," in *Sermons,* 8:41.

# EIGHT

# How Many Books Are in the Bible?

Even the most casual Bible student knows that there are more books in the Catholic Bible than in the one used by Protestants. Where did these differences originate? On what basis were some books selected to be in the Bible, and why were others rejected?

Upon reflection, we could expect that there would be some dispute regarding these matters. After all, the Bible did not come down from heaven bound in beautiful leather and adorned with gold gilded pages. It is a very human book that reflects the styles of the writers and the cultural setting of the times. Yet, it is also a divine book, inspired by God, and therefore free from error in the original manuscripts. Like Christ who was truly God and truly man, so the Bible has a dual authorship. Questions about which books meet this criterion are to be expected.

The word *canon* comes from the Greek word *kanon,* which means a ruler or measuring rod. In a metaphorical sense, it came to refer to the standard by which various books of the Bible were judged as worthy of being called the Word of God. Within time, the word *kanon* was applied to the books themselves; Athanasius is the first one known to have used "canon" in such a context.

## How the Books Were Collected

Some of the Old Testament books were immediately recognized as authoritative. Moses, after he wrote a book, put it in the Ark of the Covenant (Deut. 31:24-26). After the temple was built, the sacred writings were kept there (2 Kings 22:18). Early on, God commanded the kings to write for themselves a copy of the law. "And he shall read it all the days of his life, that he may learn to fear the Lord his God" (Deut. 17:19). As the prophets spoke God's word, saying, "Thus saith the Lord," they also recognized that their message had to be recorded for future generations.

The Jews realized that special revelation ceased with the prophet Malachi (c. 400 B.C.). In the Talmud (a handbook of Jewish traditions) we read, "Up to this point [the time of Alexander the Great] the prophets prophesied through the Holy Spirit; from this time onward incline thine ear and listen to the sayings of the wise."

But what determined whether a book was considered part of the canon? Obviously, there were other books in existence that did not merit classification with the sacred writings. Examples are "The Book of the Wars of the Lord" (Num. 21:14) and "The Book of Jashar" (Josh. 10:13).

The criterion was, first, that the book had to agree with the Torah, the first five books of Moses. But this was not the only test. Some books that agreed with the Torah were also excluded. For example, Elijah wrote a book that likely met this standard; yet it was not a part of the canon. And, of course, we must ask how the Torah itself became accepted.

Second, and most important, these books were accepted because they were believed to be inspired by God. In other words, they were selected *because they were recognized as having divine authority.* This is not to say that the Jews gave these books their authority; these books were believed to have *inherent* authority. If a book is inspired by God, it would have authority whether men recognized it or not. A jeweler may recognize an authentic diamond, but his recognition does not make it so.

We must guard against the notion that the church has a right to make a book canonical. But at best the nation Israel or church body can only *recognize* a book as authoritative because it is inspired of God.

## The Discovery of Canonicity

But how was canonicity discovered? First, the books had the ring of self-vindicating authority. Moses claimed to be the mouthpiece of God. The Old Testament prophets repeatedly said, "And the word of the Lord came to me." The lives of the prophets and the strong affirmation that their message came from God was accepted by the Jewish nation.

This explains why the canonicity of the Book of Esther was, for a time, in doubt. Since the name of God does not appear in the book, some thought it lacked self-vindicating authority. But closer inspection showed that the providence of God was so evident in the story that it had the authenticity that gave it acceptance.

A second test was that of authorship. It had to have been written by a man of God. Was the author, they asked, a spokesman for "redemptive revelation," either a prophet in the Old Testament times or an apostle in the new?

For example, Paul in the New Testament argued that his message was authoritative because he was an apostle, "not sent from men, nor through the agency of man, but through Jesus Christ, and God the Father" (Gal. 1:1). The Book of 2 Peter was disputed in the early church because some doubted that it had been written by Peter. The writing style appeared different from 1 Peter, hence the doubt. But within time the church was convinced that Peter the apostle was the author, therefore the book was accepted.

Yet in other instances the identity of the author was not

always determinative. For example, the authorship of the Book of Hebrews is unknown, but the book was accepted without serious questioning because it bears the unmistakable stamp of the transforming power of God.

Of course, the book had to be consistent with previous revelation. Martin Luther thought that James taught salvation by works so he questioned its position in the canon. Later, when he revised his preface to the book, he dropped his criticism. A closer reading indicates that James does not contradict Paul's teaching of salvation by faith. The early church was quite correct in receiving it as authoritative.

There is evidence that when an inspired book was written, it enjoyed immediate acceptance. For example, Peter accepted the epistles of Paul as being worthy of recognition as inspired Scripture (2 Pet. 3:16). Thus, the canon of the New Testament formed gradually as the books were written. Because communication was cumbersome in biblical times, it is understandable that the complete list of authoritative books was not agreed upon until a few centuries had passed. The Books of Revelation and 3 John were not immediately accepted, in part because they were unknown in some parts of the New Testament world. As their circulation grew, so did the recognition that they had the marks of divine inspiration.

The bottom line, of course, is that the books of the Bible were recognized as authoritative by the people of God. There is little doubt that we must exercise faith that God superintended his Word so that only inspired books were chosen to be in the canon. Equally important is the fact that the final list of books was not chosen by a synod or council of the church. These met to ratify the books that the people of God had already chosen.

### The Apocrypha

Both the Roman Catholic and Protestant Bibles have thirty-nine books in the Old Testament and twenty-seven

in the New. The difference is that a Roman Catholic Bible
has an additional eleven books inserted between the
Testaments. Where did these books come from?

To begin, we must realize that both branches of Christendom acknowledge the existence of books that are false
writings that have never laid serious claim to canonicity.
The Book of Enoch and The Assumption of Moses are
known to have existed, but all agree that they lack the
stamp of inspiration. In the New Testament the Shepherd
of Hermas was thought by some to be authoritative, so it
hovered around the canon for sometime before it was
dismissed as a forgery.

But there was another group of books that are accepted
by the Roman Catholic church but rejected by Protestants.
These books originated in a canon in Alexandria in Egypt.
It was in this city in 250 B.C. that the Old Testament was
translated into Greek and called the Septuagint, meaning
"seventy." (Allegedly the translation was made in seventy
days utilizing seventy scholars.) This explains why some
of the earliest manuscripts of the Septuagint that exist
today (dating back to the fourth century) contain these
additional books.

These books, commonly called the Apocrypha (the
word means "hidden"), are interwoven among the books
of the Old Testament. In all, there are fifteen books,
eleven of which are accepted as canonical by the Roman
Catholic church. But because four of the eleven are
combined with Old Testament books, the Douay Version
contains only seven additional books in its table of contents.

There are several reasons why the Roman Catholic
church considers the wider Alexandrian list of books to
be canonical. Briefly, they are (1) the New Testament
quotes mostly from the Septuagint, which contained the
Apocrypha. Then, (2) some of the early church fathers
accepted the Apocrypha as canonical—Irenaeus, Tertullian, and Clement of Alexandria for example. Also, (3)
Augustine and the great councils of Hippo and Carthage,

which he led, are said to have accepted them. Finally, (4) the Council of Trent called to respond to the inroads of the Reformation pronounced them canonical in A.D. 1546. The council said that if anyone does not receive these books in all of their parts, "let him be anathema."

## Reasons to Reject the Apocrypha

Protestants give numerous reasons for rejecting these additional books:[1]

1. Though there are some allusions to the apocryphal books by New Testament writers (Hebrews 11:35 compares with 2 Maccabees 7, 12) there is no direct quote from them. Also, no New Testament writer ever refers to any of these fourteen or fifteen books as authoritative. Quotes from the accepted books are usually introduced by the phrase, "It is written," or the passage is quoted to prove a point. But never do the New Testament writers quote the Apocrypha in this way.

2. There is no evidence that the books were in the Septuagint as early as the time of Christ. Remember, the earliest manuscripts that have them date back to the fourth century A.D. Even if they were in the Septuagint at this early date, it is noteworthy that neither Christ nor the apostles ever quoted from them.

3. Though some of the early leaders of the church accepted them, many did not—Athanasius, Origen, and Jerome, to name a few.

4. The evidence that Augustine accepted the Apocrypha is at best ambiguous. For one thing, he omits Baruch and includes 1 Esdras, thus accepting one and rejecting another in contrast to the Council of Trent. For another, he seemed to change his mind later about the validity of the Apocrypha.

Jerome, while making a Latin translation of the Bible, disputed with Augustine about the value of these additional books. Though Jerome did not want to translate them, he eventually made a hurried translation of them but kept them separate from his translation of the Bible. However, after his death, these books were brought into his Latin translation.

Augustine, as mentioned, argued in favor of the Apocrypha, though he later seemed to give them a kind of secondary canonicity. His testimony, though important, is not entirely clear.

5. Even the Roman Catholic church made a distinction between the Apocrypha and the other books of the Bible prior to the Reformation. For example, Cardinal Cajetan, who opposed Luther at Augsburg, in 1518 published *A Commentary on all the Authentic Historical Books of the Old Testament.* His commentary, however, did not include the Apocrypha.

6. The first official council of the Roman Catholic church to ratify these books was at the Council of Trent in 1546, only twenty-nine years after Luther posted his ninety-five theses on the door of the church at Wittenberg. The acceptance of these books at this time was convenient since the books were being quoted against Luther. For example, 2 Maccabees speaks of prayers for the dead (2 Macc. 12:45-46) and another book teaches salvation by works (Tob. 12:19).

Even so, the Roman church accepted only eleven of the fifteen books; we naturally would expect that these books, since they were together for so many centuries, would be either accepted or rejected together.

7. The content of the Apocrypha is sub-biblical. Some of the stories are clearly fanciful. Bel and the Dragon, Tobit, and Judith have the earmarks of legend; the authors of these books even give hints along the way that the stories are not to be taken seriously.

What is more, these books have historical errors. It is claimed that Tobit was alive when the Assyrians conquered Israel in 722 B.C. and also when Jeroboam revolted against Judah in 931 B.C., which would make him at least 209 years old; yet according to the account, he died when he was only 158 years. The Book of Judith speaks of Nebuchadnezzar reigning in Nineveh instead of Babylon.

These inaccuracies are inconsistent with the doctrine of inspiration which teaches that when God inspires a book it is free from all errors.

8. Finally, and most important, we must remember that the Apocrypha was never part of the Old Testament Hebrew canon. When Christ was on earth, he frequently quoted from the Old Testament but never from the Apocryphal books because they were never a part of the Hebrew canon.

In Christ's time, there were twenty-two books in the Old Testament, but the content was identical to the thirty-nine books in our present Old Testament (several of the books in the Hebrew Bible were combined, which accounts for the different figure). Genesis was the first book in the Hebrew canon and 2 Chronicles was the last. On at least one occasion, Christ referred specifically to the content of the Hebrew canon when he said:

*Therefore, behold, I am sending you prophets and wise men and scribes; some of them you will kill and crucify, and some of them you will scourge in your synagogues, and persecute from city to city, that upon you may fall the guilt of all the righteous blood shed on earth, from the blood of righteous Abel to the blood of Zechariah, the son of Berechiah, whom you murdered between the temple and the altar. (Matt. 23:34-35)*

In the Hebrew canon, the first book of the Bible was Genesis, where the death of Abel is recorded, and the last book was 2 Chronicles where near the end of the book the murder of Zechariah is described (24:21). In between these two events lay the entire content of the Old Testament. He assumed it ended with the Hebrew Scriptures and not the Apocrypha.

The Apocryphal books were written in Greek after the close of the Old Testament canon. Jewish scholars agree that chronologically Malachi was the last book of the Old Testament canon. The books of the Apocrypha were evidently written about 200 B.C. and occur only in Greek manuscripts of the Old Testament. Since Christ accepted only the books we have in our Old Testament today, we have no reason to add to their number.

## The Lost Books

Occasionally we hear references to the so-called lost books of the Bible, books that some people think have been hidden from the general populace. In 1979, Bell Publishing Company of New York came out with a book entitled *The Lost Books of the Bible.* On the flyleaf it says that these books were not among those chosen to comprise the Bible, and "They were suppressed by the church, and for over fifteen hundred years were shrouded in secrecy."[2]

These books are not really as secret as the authors imply. New Testament scholars have been well aware of their existence throughout the centuries, though perhaps these books were not accessible to the common man. Their credibility is rejected by both Catholics and Protestants.

These books include stories about the birth of Mary and of Christ. Also there are a dozen or more stories that took place during Christ's lifetime. Three or four purport to relate to events in the Old Testament.

These books never even vied for a place in the canon. Unlike some other books that were actually disputed (the Shepherd of Hermas, for example), these books were recognized as legends from the beginning. These "forgotten books" are so obviously inferior to those in our Bible that they cannot be taken seriously.

Indeed, in the preface, Dr. Frank Crane admitted the

point by saying that legends and apocryphal stories surround all great men such as Napoleon, Charlemagne, and Julius Caesar, so we can also expect that tales would grow up around Christ. He went on to say that Christ appealed to the "fictional minds" of his day. These writers, Crane admitted, do not pretend to write down what is strictly true, but tinge all events with their imagination.

Finally, Crane said the common man can now make his own decision as to whether the early church did right in rejecting these books. He did not hesitate to say that common sense itself will show the superiority of the accepted canonical books.

I agree. Should there be any doubt about the accepted books, the best solution would be to read these so-called lost books. And for that matter, one should also read those books that laid more serious claim to canonicity. They also are so inferior to the books of the New Testament that we become convinced that the early church did not err.

In the upper room, Christ promised that the Holy Spirit would help them recall his teachings. "When the Helper comes, whom I will send to you from the Father, that is the Spirit of truth, who proceeds from the Father, He will bear witness of Me" (John 15:26). That was a tacit confirmation of the New Testament that still needed to be written. The early believers recognized those writings that were either written by an apostle or by someone personally acquainted with one. After the apostolic period, no more books could claim the stamp of divine authority.

The Book of Revelation ends with a warning:

*I testify to everyone who hears the words of the prophecy of this book: if anyone adds to them, God shall add to him the plagues which are written in this book; and if anyone takes away from the words of the book of this prophecy, God shall take away his part from the tree of*

*life and from the holy city, which are written in this
book. (Rev. 22:18-19)*

Although these words refer specifically to the Book of
Revelation and not to the New Testament as a whole
(there were still questions as to which books were properly in the New Testament when Revelation was penned),
yet they are a warning to the many false cults who have
claimed to add to God's Word.

In our present New Testament we have the final word
from God until our Lord returns and the Bible as we know
it will no longer be necessary.

*Notes*

1. Norman Geisler and William Nix, *A General Introduction to the
   Bible* (Chicago: Moody Press, 1986), 170-177.
2. *The Lost Books of the Bible* (New York: Bell Publishing Co., 1979).

# NINE

# Predestination or Free Will: Augustine v. Pelagius

Perhaps you heard about the group of theologians who were discussing the doctrines of predestination and free will. When the argument became heated, the dissidents split into two groups. One man, unable to make up his mind which group to join, slipped into the predestination crowd. Challenged as to why he was there, he replied, "I came of my own free will."

The group retorted, "Free will! You don't belong here!"

So he retreated to the opposing group and when asked why he switched responded, "I was sent here."

"Get out," they stormed. "You can't join us unless you come of your own free will!" The confused man was left out in the cold.

Ask the average twentieth-century Christian whether he sees himself in the predestination crowd versus the free-will crowd and he will probably join the man who was left out in the cold! Our age is not given to serious theological reflection. In a day of pop religion, speculation about the freedom of the will and predestination seems pointless. Yet to the greatest theological minds in the history of the church, one's answer to this question determined whether or not he understood the gospel.

In the early part of the fifth century, this question, with

all of its implications, was the subject of hot debate. It all began when a British monk by the name of Pelagius took exception to a statement made by Augustine, the great theologian of the North African city of Hippo.

The remark that triggered the controversy was, of all things, a line in a prayer by Augustine, who was profoundly aware of his own sinfulness. Convinced that he was entirely helpless in the sight of God, he cried, "O God, command what you will, but give what you command." Augustine's point was simply that if God expected anything from him, God would have to grant what was expected. Of himself, Augustine was too bound by sin to keep even the most basic of God's commands.

Augustine's father was a heathen, his mother, Monica, an eager Christian. Despite their poverty, they were able to give him a good education, first near home, then in Carthage, the capital of North Africa. There Augustine fell into moral sin and begat an illegitimate son, Adeodatus. Later he left his mistress and found himself in "a whirl of vicious lovemaking." Because he could not control his passions, he was tormented by guilt and moral helplessness.

One day he was introduced to Christianity through the preaching of Ambrose, a bishop of the church. He envied those who appeared to be able to master their passions; his interest in Christianity was stirred. One day while walking in a garden in Milan he heard a child say, "Take it and read it." He picked up his New Testament and his eyes fell on a passage perfectly suited to his life-style: "Let us behave properly as in the day, not in carousing and drunkenness, not in sexual promiscuity and sensuality, not in strife and jealousy. But put on the Lord Jesus Christ, and make no provision for the flesh in regard to its lusts" (Rom. 13:13-14). At that moment the light of peace came to his heart, and he was converted. He never forgot how completely he had been a slave to sin before his conversion.

Pelagius, the British monk, had no such sense of helplessness. He was well-disciplined, a student of Greek theology, and believed that with some help from God man could better himself. In about 409, he came to Rome and wrote a commentary on Paul's epistles. He converted a young theologian by the name of Celestius to his view that man was capable on his own to keep any command God gave him. It would be inconsistent for God to give man a command he couldn't obey. When Christ said, "Be ye perfect even as your Father in heaven is perfect," Pelagius believed that Christ would not have given such a command if it were beyond achievement. He eloquently extolled the virtues of man and his inherent ability to do God's will. "As often as I have to speak concerning moral improvement and the leading of a holy life, I am accustomed first to set forth the power and quality of human nature and to show what it can accomplish."[1]

The cornerstone of Pelagius's theory was the freedom of the will. When faced with a choice of whether to sin or not to sin, man can choose one direction or another. To quote Pelagius, man has "the absolutely equal ability at every moment to do good or evil."[2] Therefore, man can, if he so wishes, live sinlessly. If we could not keep every one of God's commands, he would be unfair in giving them. Pelagius's slogan was, "Whatever I ought to do, I can do."

Both Pelagius and Augustine agreed that Adam was created morally neutral and so chose freely when he sinned. But Pelagius went on to maintain that Adam's fall hurt only himself and no one else. Children do not have original sin, nor are they born under the condemnation of Adam's sin. They are born neutral and, theoretically at least, have the ability to live sinlessly. As might be expected, Augustine disagreed with these conclusions.

Celestius, the pupil of Pelagius, asserted the following:

1. Adam was created mortal and would have died even if he had not sinned.
2. Adam's fall injured himself alone, not the human race.

3. Children come into the world in the same condition in which Adam was before the fall.
4. The human race neither dies because of Adam's fall, nor rises again because of Christ's resurrection.
5. Unbaptized children, as well as others, are saved.
6. The law, as well as the gospel, leads to the kingdom of heaven.
7. Even before Christ's death there were sinless men.[3]

Under questioning, Celestius returned evasive answers, declaring these propositions to be speculative. Yet he also refused to admit that these statements were erroneous.

Did Pelagius and Celestius believe that the grace of God was unnecessary? Not at all. Even though they believed that God did not have to intervene directly in the human soul to save a person, they taught that man's natural ability to keep God's commands was in itself an expression of God's grace. Pelagius attributed man's ability to live without sin to the "necessity of nature." Thus God's grace is displayed through human freedom.

Since Adam's sin injured only himself, children today are born just as neutral as Adam was before the Fall. In many cases they grow up and live without sin, and if they do transgress, they can return to God, receive his forgiveness, and henceforth perfectly obey his commandments. Some men, Pelagius taught, had no need to repeat the petition in the Lord's Prayer, "Forgive us our trespasses." Obviously, they could be saved without the gospel. Since they can fully obey the law of God on their own, the necessity of grace as a supernatural gift was denied.

Pelagius did still affirm the necessity of baptizing infants, even though his own views would render it unnecessary. Why should infants be baptized if they are not sinners? Celestius answered that they should not be baptized for the forgiveness of sins, but that they might be "sanctified in Christ." But why should they have to be sanctified in Christ if they are not born under the condem-

nation of sin? Later, on May 1, 418, at the Synod of Carthage, this inconsistency was pointed out. Standing against
Pelagianism, this council affirmed, "Anyone who denies
that newborn infants are to be baptized for the remission
of sins, let him be anathema."

It should be remembered that freedom of the will for
Pelagius had nothing to do with the question of whether
we are free to choose pancakes instead of eggs for break-
fast. That question is interesting but beside the point.
Pelagius meant that man was free to obey the commandments of God. He was not helplessly bound by sin. Whatever God commands us to do *we can do.* As we shall see,
Pelagianism was vigorously condemned by Augustine and
subsequent church councils. But we must credit Pelagius
with raising a question that will be debated for centuries:
If man does not have freedom of the will, how can God
hold him accountable for his actions?

## Augustine

Next to the Apostle Paul, the one man who has had the
greatest influence on the theology of Christendom was
Augustine. He himself experienced both the agony of guilt
and the joy of forgiveness. Multiplied millions have read
his *Confessions,* the personal thoughts of a man who is
coming to grips with his sinfulness in the presence of
God. On the first page is the famous statement, "O Lord,
Thou hast made us for thyself and our hearts are restless
until they find their all in thee."

By the time Pelagius began writing theology, Augustine
was already fifty-seven years old; his doctrine was already
settled. However, Augustine believed that Pelagianism was
a threat to the very heart of the gospel and therefore
wrote extensively against this heresy.

Augustine believed that Adam was created with the
ability not to sin, but because of the Fall, sin was now
inevitable. No man, of himself, had the freedom to live

righteously. What is even more obvious is that man cannot change his own heart.

Augustine believed that infants are born into the world under the condemnation of Adam's sin. They not only are born with this original sin, but they have a corrupt nature and hence lack the ability to fulfill the commands of God. If men are saved, it is because of the direct intervention of God. The regeneration of the soul must be the exclusive and supernatural work of the Holy Spirit. Salvation is by grace alone. As the American theologian William Shedd writes, "Grace is imparted to sinful man, not because he believes, but in order that he may believe; for faith itself is a gift of God."

Even personal experience teaches that we do not have freedom of the will as Pelagius believed. We lack the ability to make righteous choices because our wills are a slave to sin. Whereas the battle cry of Pelagius was, "I ought therefore I can," Augustine cried out in despair, "I ought but I cannot."

If, therefore, man is so sinful that he cannot cooperate in his own salvation, the question arises, Why are some men saved and others not? The answer, according to Augustine, is that God has predestined some men to eternal life. God gives to these both the desire and the ability to believe on Christ; they do so because of God's choice—not their own. As for those who are not saved, they are predestined to damnation.

This doctrine of double predestination affirmed that God could have justly chosen not to save anyone; so the salvation of a single individual is solely because of God's grace. Yet Augustine frequently admitted that God's sovereign grace is a mystery that we cannot understand. He often repeated Paul's words:

*Oh the depth of the riches both of the wisdom and knowledge of God! How unsearchable are His judgments and unfathomable His ways! . . . For from Him and through*

*Him and to Him are all things. To Him be the glory
forever. Amen. (Rom. 11:33-36)*

We can't discern God's reasons for saving whom he
wills.

To Augustine, man's will was not free as Pelagius had
taught. If Pelagius were right, then man might in some
way thwart the purposes of God. But because the human
will is under the direction of God, his purpose is certain
to be accomplished. "However strong the wills of either
angels or of men, whether they will what God wills or will
something else, the will of the omnipotent is always
undefeated."

Augustine, then, believed that the unconverted did not
have freedom of the will, but Christians did—at least they
had the ability to choose the right. Because God has given
them the Holy Spirit, they have the ability to do what they
ought. Freedom means that they are given grace that
compensates for their sinfulness. As the law is established
by faith, so free will is established by grace. Grace cures
the will so that it loves righteousness.

Why does God command sinners to do what they
cannot? "But God commands something which we cannot
do, in order that we may know what we ought to ask of
him." [4]

Pelagius had defined freedom of the will as the ability
to choose between right and wrong, and he believed that
man had this ability. Augustine disagreed, believing that
man's will was bound in sin. For him freedom of the will
meant that a saved man had the ability to do the right.

## A Summary

Clearly, Pelagianism and Augustinianism are in sharp
opposition to one another. Several observations come to
mind in summarizing the progress of the debate so far.
First, we can see how doctrines are interrelated. When

Pelagius came to believe in human ability, he diminished the need for God's grace. When Augustine concluded that man was so deeply fallen that his will was in bondage to sin, he magnified the need for sovereign grace. As we shall see, one belief, whether true or false, often dictates the fabric of a whole theological system.

Second, we can see the profound influence of one man in the history of Christian thought. From Augustine two theological streams seep into the doctrine of subsequent centuries. The Reformers, such as Luther and Calvin, quote him with approval as they develop the biblical doctrine of salvation, which had become lost in medieval times. The Roman Catholics will use him to support their view of the church (a matter already discussed in a previous chapter).

As might be expected, Pelagianism was condemned by the church, but Augustinianism was not wholly accepted either. Human nature resists the idea that God makes the choice as to who will be saved and who will be lost. Thus a mediating position was eventually adopted that tried to combine these two diverse systems of theology.

### Semi-Pelagianism

Augustine's view of double predestination and the irresistibility of grace was not welcomed in some theological circles. Some theologians believed it led to fatalism. They accused Augustine of saying, "By God's predestination men are compelled to sin and driven to death by a sort of fatal necessity." What is more, logically Augustine would have to assert that God wills evil.

As a result, some theologians tried to take the best of the two extremes. Man did indeed become corrupted though the Fall, but his reasoning powers were largely unaffected. Salvation was therefore of grace, but man could cooperate with God in salvation.

These men asserted that the sovereignty of God and the

free will of man stood together in an antinomy—that is, they were only apparently in contradiction to each other. Augustine had resolved the dilemma in favor of grace and thus had to deny human freedom; Pelagius had resolved it in favor of human freedom and denied grace. Semi-Pelagianism promised to avoid both errors.

Surely there could be a middle path by which one could affirm the need for both freedom and grace. How could the call to repentance be given unless all men could be saved? If only the elect could be saved, the invitation to all men would be superfluous. In fact, if the elect are going to be saved by the predetermined will of God, why even bother to evangelize unbelievers?

So semi-Pelagianism taught that there was room for grace alongside of free will. For one thing, God sent Christ to die for the sins of the world; for another, he graciously gave man a free will by which the gift of salvation could be accepted or rejected. This natural ability of man is also a gift of grace. The fact that God has planted these seeds of goodness in man does not detract from the wonder of redemption. To praise the free will of man is to praise his Creator.

There was another point in favor of this moderate view. Augustine found it difficult to explain how man could be responsible if his will was not free. After all, if it was man's nature to sin, how could man be judged for doing what he did naturally? We do not blame a chicken for sprouting feathers because such an action is natural to it. If man is totally corrupt, how can he be guilty for doing what is consistent with his nature? Only if he was free to do otherwise could he be accountable.

Although Semi-Pelagianism was condemned point by point at the Council of Orange in A.D. 529, it eventually became the position of the Roman Catholic church. Today it is also widely accepted by evangelicals who teach that it is man, not God, who makes the choice as to whether an individual is saved. The impression is given that God would like to save many more than are being saved, but he cannot because he does not violate the free will of man.

Some say that the Bible teaches Semi-Pelagianism in passages such as 1 Timothy 2:4, where Paul said that God "desires all men to be saved and to come to the knowledge of the truth." This statement is interpreted to mean that God could not possibly have predestinated some to damnation. What is more, God would like to save everyone, but his power is limited because of man's free will.

For many, Semi-Pelagianism is a satisfying halfway house between the extremes of Pelagius and Augustine. Yes, salvation is of grace, but whether it is received or rejected depends on man's will. When he receives the free gift of salvation he cooperates with God in salvation.

But for others, Semi-Pelagianism would not answer some tough questions about the purposes and power of God. The debate was far from over.

Let's move on to round Number Two.

## Notes

1. Cited in Philip Schaff, *History of the Christian Church* (n.p., n.d.), 3:322.
2. Ibid.
3. Ibid., 322-323.
4. Roger Hazelton, ed., *Selected Writings of Saint Augustine* (Cleveland: The World Publishing Co., 1982), 209.

# TEN

# Predestination or Free Will: Luther v. Erasmus

You have probably participated in a discussion about predestination versus free will and concluded that the matter was either too complex or else irrelevant. Since there are fine Christians on both sides of the issues, you may be tempted to conclude that the controversy is really not all that important.

Martin Luther has a word for you. He said that those people who are not interested in this issue "shall know nothing whatever of Christian matters and shall be far behind all the people of the earth. He that does not feel this, let him confess that he is no Christian."[1] Strong words!

Why did Martin Luther believe this issue was so essential? He was convinced that it went to the heart of the gospel. It was the "hinge" on which everything turns. *To affirm free will was to compromise grace.*

You have had the experience of pulling a loose thread in a sock and having it all come unraveled. What appeared to be a minor problem turned out to have hidden connections. So the question of free will directly affects all theology.

In the Reformation era, the Pelagian-Augustinian con-

troversy erupted with renewed vigor. The Dutch humanist
Erasmus of Rotterdam wrote a book critical of Luther's
strong support of Augustine's views that the will was not
free. The book, entitled *Diatribe concerning Free Will,*
begins with Erasmus acknowledging that he will be
criticized for attacking Luther—like a fly trying to attack
an elephant. But he professed great respect for Luther and
believed Luther would welcome this exchange of views.
Erasmus didn't think the issue was very important, but it
was at least worthy of consideration. So in the book he
presented several arguments showing the rational and
biblical support for free will.

Luther countered with a thunderous denunciation of
Erasmus in his book *The Bondage of the Will.* Undoubtedly, it is Luther's best work (he himself said so) and thus
deserves careful study. To read Luther is to grasp the
drama, wit, and passion of lively theological dialogue.
These matters that impinge on salvation and damnation
touched a nerve that resulted in a brilliant defense of the
gospel.

Luther and Erasmus had been friends—indeed Erasmus
had paved the way for Luther's reforms by publishing a
new edition of the Greek New Testament. "Erasmus laid
the egg and Luther hatched it," the historians tell us. But
this debate ended their friendship. Luther considered
Erasmus's arguments to be weak and inconsistent. "Erasmus," Luther wrote, "is an eel. Only Christ can grab him."

One writer who borrowed an image of another day
described their conflict. "It was a duel in which the two
participants got up at the crack of dawn, one armed with a
rapier, the other with a blunderbuss, where shaking of
fists and mutterings usurped the place of battle, and
which ended with the two antagonists going their separate
ways, undamaged but shaken, and with a frustrating sense
of horror ruffled but unsatisfied."[2]

A few preliminary matters are necessary to give the
discussion perspective. First of all, the question is not
whether men have freedom of choice in matters pertain-

ing to everyday life. Luther could not care less about whether a man has the freedom to choose to lie out in the sun or to stay indoors. Such a discussion, though interesting, has nothing to do with the gospel. At stake is the question of whether man can, *on his own,* turn away from sin to God. Second, Luther and Erasmus are talking about the willpower of the unconverted. They do not address the question of whether a Christian has free will in these matters. Since believers are indwelt by the Holy Spirit, it is reasonable to suppose that they are able to exercise freedom in spiritual matters, even as Augustine believed.

The debate, then, centers on whether the unconverted person can make any contribution whatever to his salvation, whether he has by nature the ability to take any step toward God on his own, or whether God sovereignly quickens those who are dead in trespasses and sins and moves their will to receive the truth of the gospel.

Erasmus wanted to say that man, though fallen, can contribute to his salvation; Luther argued that man is passive in salvation, that it is a sovereign work of God. Though the distinction appears slight, it impinges on our understanding of the gospel message.

Erasmus defines free choice in a way reminiscent of Pelagius. "By free choice in this place we mean a power of the human will by which a man can apply himself to the things which lead to eternal salvation, or to turn away from them."[3] Yes, grace is necessary for salvation, but man has power to initiate his relationship with God. He chooses God; God does not choose him.

What effect did the Fall have on man's natural powers? Erasmus said man is weakened; his powers are considerably impaired, but he is not wholly carnal. His nature possesses some capacity for knowledge and obedience to God. Thus, man can at least say that he has made some contribution toward his eternal salvation. Man and God are partners in redemption, though admittedly man's part is rather small.

Luther saw this as a cheapening of grace. Even admitting

that man can merit grace by exercising freedom of choice diminishes the grace of God. If Erasmus is right, one man is converted and another is lost because there is a difference in men; the former had the good sense to exercise his free will and choose Christ, while the latter did not. Luther wanted to say that one man is saved and another is lost because *God alone made the difference among them.* All men are equally bound in sin. Thus if one believes, it is because God chose him to salvation and wrought special grace in his heart to bring it about.

Was Luther just being stubborn on a technical point? Or was the heart of the gospel at stake as he claimed? Let us follow the argument to find out.


## Freedom or Bondage?

Luther assailed Erasmus for saying that this debate was not very important. He believed his former friend was so far off base that he wanted to make him repent for having published his *Diatribe.* Erasmus was diluting the pure teaching of Scripture by his obtuse reasoning, but it was like trying to put out fire with straw!

Erasmus said that if Luther's position that men are bound was generally known, it would open a floodgate of iniquity, presumably because men would say that they are not to be blamed for their evil. Luther countered by saying that if God has revealed that it is so, then who was Erasmus to complain? "What, shall your Creator come to learn of you his creature, what is useful and what is not useful to be preached?" If God willed that such things should be spoken of and proclaimed without regard for what would follow, who was Erasmus to forbid it?

When Erasmus asked who would endeavor to amend his life if he thought everything happened by necessity, Luther replied, "No man! No man can. Except, of course, the elect. Who will believe he is loved of God? No man can! But the elect shall believe it."

Luther was content to know that God had promised grace to the humble. In fact, we cannot be thoroughly humbled until we realize we cannot do anything toward our own salvation. Consider the full impact of his words:

*But man cannot be thoroughly humbled, until he comes to know that his salvation is utterly beyond his own powers, counsel, endeavors, will, and works, and absolutely depending on the will, counsel, pleasure, and work of another, that is, on God only. For if, as long as he has any persuasion that he can do even the least thing himself toward his own salvation, he retains a confidence in himself and does not utterly despair in himself, so long he is not humbled before God; but he proposes to himself some place, some time, or some work, whereby he may at length attain unto salvation. But he who hesitates not to depend wholly upon the good-will of God, he totally despairs in himself, chooses nothing for himself but waits for God to work in him; and such an one is the nearest unto grace, that he might be saved.*[4]

Luther's point was that the doctrine of sovereign grace crushes the pride of man. When this doctrine is preached and man grasps it, he casts himself helplessly upon God's mercy. So he continued:

*These things, therefore are openly proclaimed for the Elect: that being by these means humbled and brought down to nothing, they might be saved. The rest resist this humiliation; nay, they condemn the teaching of self-desperation; they have a little something that they may do themselves. These secretly remain proud, and adversaries to the grace of God.*[5]

What is really at stake here? Many evangelicals today teach that salvation is by God's grace, but God looks to the sinner to contribute the faith by which he may be saved; man chooses God; God does not choose man. So there is at least something, however small, that God looks to man for in salvation. This popular conception of the gospel was taught by Erasmus.

Luther strongly disagreed. He would say that *even the faith by which a man believes is God-given.* Of course, man's will is involved in salvation, but it is God acting on the will that causes the man to seek God. Therefore a person is saved not because he had of himself the desire or ability to believe but because God chose him and acted on his will to bring him to faith. For Luther, salvation was wholly of the Lord.

Erasmus produced his own set of arguments to counter Luther's objections.

### The Debate

1. Erasmus cited dozens of passages from the Old Testament in which God commanded people to choose righteousness. "Turn ye unto Me," the Lord declares. Erasmus assumed that whatever God commands man to do, man *can* do. If it were otherwise, he imagined one praying to God:

*Why do you promise upon condition what is decided by your own will? ... Why do you reproach when it is not in my power to guard what you have given me, or to exclude the ill you sent into me? Why do you entreat when it all depends on your good pleasure? Why do you bless as though I have performed a good work when whatever is done is your work? Why do you curse if I have sinned by necessity? What end do all the myriad of commandments serve if it is not possible for a man in any way to keep what is commanded?*[6]

Luther responded by saying that it is but human reason to infer free will just because God gives men commandments. God knew full well that man could never keep the commandments—the fact that we are told to love the Lord our God with all our heart does not mean we are capable of it. Satan's work is to hold men so that they never become aware of their wretchedness, and he wants them to presume they are capable of all that God requires. Human nature is blind, so that it does not know its own strength—or rather, sickness; moreover being proud, it thinks it can do everything. God can cure this pride and ignorance by the publication of his law. God knew we couldn't keep it and wants us to agree.

Luther vividly described the state of the natural man as "bound, miserable, captive, sick, and dead, but who by the operation of his lord, Satan, adds to his other miseries, blindness: so that he believes he is free, happy, at liberty, powerful, whole and alive." For such there is only one hope, namely, that he might see his utter need of divine grace. The Apostle Paul taught that the law was given not because it could be kept, but that it might drive us to Christ (Gal. 3:22-27). Erasmus erred when he thought that the natural man can do what his God commands him to do. He confused law and grace.

Why does God give commandments that are impossible for man to keep? *To drive man to despair that he might cast himself upon the mercy of God.* With Augustine, Luther shouted, "I ought, but I cannot!"

2. Erasmus quoted the words of Christ in Matthew 23:37, "O Jerusalem, Jerusalem, who kills the prophets and stones those who are sent to her! How often I wanted to gather your children together, the way a hen gathers her chicks under her wings, and you were unwilling." Erasmus asked:

*If all is determined by necessity, could not Jerusalem rightly reply to the Lord who weeps over it "Why do you torment yourself with vain tears? If you did not wish us to listen to the prophets, why did you send them to us?*

*Why impute to us what has been done by your will and our necessity? You wished us to be gathered together, but at the same time wished us not to do so, for you have worked in us what we did not wish ourselves.*[7]

Luther replied that God Incarnate was sent for the specific purpose of offering salvation to all men; but he also offends many who are abandoned or hardened by God's secret will of majesty; thus they do not receive him.

Luther at this point made a distinction that was important to his theology: There is the revealed will of God and the secret, hidden purpose of God. On the one hand, God pleads with the sinner to believe; yet, on the other hand, he plans the damnation of many. This secret will is not to be inquired into but to be reverently adored. We should not ask why it is so but rather stand in awe of God.

Did Luther have biblical justification for such a "secret will of God" that differs from his revealed will? Paul in Romans 9 made such an appeal when pressed with the question as to how God can hold man accountable if in fact man's will is hardened by the Almighty. An objector, such as Erasmus, upon hearing that God has mercy on some but hardens others, might ask, "Why does He still find fault? For who resists his will?" Paul had a perfect opportunity here to say that God finds fault simply because man has a free will and has the power to choose God but does not do so. Instead, he replied:

*On the contrary, who are you, O man, who answers back to God? The thing molded will not say to the molder, "Why did you make me like this," will it? Or does not the potter have a right over the clay, to make from the same lump one vessel for honorable use, and another for common use? (Romans 9:20-21)*

The clay has no right to question the potter. We have no permission to pry into the secret counsels of the Almighty, but to put our hands over our mouths. As Luther said, all we can do is to stand in awe of God.

Luther might have used the case of Abraham to make his point. God telling Abraham to slay his son was an expression of the revealed will of God; but at the same time, God was secretly planning that the boy would live. Thus, God may make certain commands but be planning something contrary to what he commanded. In other words, we must not think we can read God's ultimate intentions. (More about this in the next chapter.)

Luther's answer was a reply to the Semi-Pelagians, who made use of 1 Timothy 2:4: "God desires all men to be saved." Simply put, Luther would say that God may desire the salvation of all men but had chosen to forgo those desires for a higher, hidden purpose. If the salvation of all men was his overriding priority, he could prevent Satan from blinding the eyes of the unconverted so that more would believe. He would work toward the softening, not the hardening, of all men.

Beyond this, Luther was not willing to go. If someone wished to pry into God's secret will, he might choose to do so at his own peril. Luther wrote, "We let him go on and, like the giants, fight against God; while we look on to see what triumph he will gain, persuaded in ourselves that he will do nothing, either to injure our cause or advance his own."[8]

Can such a view of God be reconciled with the mercy of God? Luther wrote, "This is the highest degree of faith—to believe that he is merciful, who saves so few and damns so many." That God displays mercy to the elect is clear enough. But as Paul said, "So then He has mercy on whom He desires, and He hardens whom He desires" (Rom. 9:18).

When Christ pled with the inhabitants of Jerusalem, we see the *revealed* will of God. Yet, the secret will of God was that the people not believe. God apparently had some ultimate purpose for displaying mercy to some and hardening others.

3. Erasmus attempted to deal with some of the passages that contradict the notion of free will. He explained the

case of the hardening of Pharaoh by saying that his evil deeds made him obstinate and God increased his evil that he should be brought to repentance. "Just as by the action of the same sun, wax melts and mud hardens, so the forbearance of God that tolerates the sinner brings some to repentance and makes others more obstinate in wrong-doing."

Luther replied that for Erasmus everything was thrown "topsy-turvy." When God says, "I will harden Pharaoh's heart," Erasmus changes the person to read, "Pharaoh hardens his own heart." The figure of the wax and mud does not apply, since the point at hand is whether God himself determines whether a man's heart is clay or mud. Clearly, God did not harden Pharaoh's heart to bring him to repentance, but that he might resist the request of Moses. In fact, Paul clearly taught that God did not show mercy to Pharaoh, lest he be brought to repentance (Rom. 9:17).

Luther admitted, of course, that we should not think that God directly wrought evil in Pharaoh's heart. God simply commands the evil will to do what it does naturally. For example, David said of Shemei, "If he curses, and if the Lord has told him, 'Curse David,' then who shall say, 'Why have you done so?' " (2 Sam. 16:10). Though God himself would not curse, the good God by means of an evil, blaspheming instrument commands these evil words.

The Lord could have used the devil to do the hardening. As in the case of Saul, an evil spirit from the Lord troubled him. Yes, God caused the evil, though he did not do it directly but commanded that it be done.

To summarize, Luther said that the will of the unconverted is captive to the evil desires of the heart and to Satan, for Paul wrote that we should warn people to escape from the snare of the devil, "having been held captive by him to do his will" (2 Tim. 2:26). In contrast, the will of the converted is captive to God who wrought salvation in their hearts.

Luther continued, the human will is like a beast—if

God sits on it, it goes where God wills; if Satan sits on it, it goes where Satan wills. The beast, however, lacks the ability to choose its own rider. The riders themselves strive to see who shall ride on the beast's back.

Yet Luther did not believe that God forces a man to do evil. When he spoke of a man doing evil by necessity, he did not mean that God takes a man and overpowers him like a thief might do. Rather, men do evil "spontaneously and with a desirous willingness." Thus, to harden a man's heart, God may have to do no more than simply to abandon him to his own desires and lusts. Yet such an action by God does render the man's sinful actions as necessary.

And when God works in the heart of the elect to bring them to faith, it is also not coercion, but "the will, being changed and sweetly breathed on by the Spirit of God, desires and acts not from *compulsion,* but *responsively,* from pure willingness, inclination, and accord."[9]

The bottom line, however, is that the will of man is not free, but responsive to either the wickedness of the heart or the sovereign work of God, which grants to some the ability to believe the gospel.

### What Is at Stake?

How important was this dispute between Luther and Erasmus in the history of the Reformation? The Roman Catholic church regarded the freedom of the will *the central issue* in Luther's split with the church.

In a recent article, Roman Catholic scholar Thomas Molar said that Luther's views are incompatible with Catholicism because of his view of man. He cited as proof Luther's insistence that man is infinitely weak, his will is captive and strangled by evil appetites that can reach out for nothing good. Molar correctly sees that for Luther the origin of faith is divine election. Thus God's elective grace precedes man's faith. Hence no merit, no good works, no interceding saints.

Molar assailed Luther's views as war against humanity.

But he did admit that Luther was totally consistent. Unlike
the eclectics who attempt to build a theological system
on both human merit and divine grace, Luther had a
coherence that we can admire. "Once the principle was
laid down that the greatness of God supposed the nothing-
ness of man, man could not be raised up again without
God."[10]

In contrast to Luther, Roman Catholicism holds that
man is not totally depraved; the Fall made man morally
sick but not dead. Man can contribute to his own salvation
by preparing his heart to receive grace and by cooperating
with God in the salvation process. And, as we learned in
previous chapters, because man can cooperate with God
in salvation, good works become indispensable in the
quest for eternal life. Cardinal Bernardin of Chicago,
when contrasting the Catholic view of conversion with
the evangelical position, said, "We see conversion as an
ongoing reality." The reason is because man is in continual
cooperation with God in the work of salvation, a work
that is never finished.

Evangelicals differ with the Catholic church by asserting
that salvation is a free gift and that the conversion experience happens at a point in time. However, there is this
similarity: many evangelicals believe that God looks to
man for the faith needed to believe the gospel. And the
choice as to who will be saved or lost is made by men, not
God. Luther, and Calvin, whom we shall consider in the
next chapter, disagreed.

Perhaps the two views can be contrasted like this:
Catholicism and much of evangelicalism today views man
as drowning, and God in grace throws him a rope. But
whether or not the man grabs it depends on his own
choice and disposition. And even after he has grasped the
rope, he must, by his own efforts, hang onto it. Luther saw
man as drowning but totally unaware of it because he was,
spiritually speaking, dead. Hence he could not even reach
out to God's grace. God, by his own choice, has to reach

down and save man. He does this by quickening the lifeless corpses and granting him the faith to believe. Thus salvation is wholly of God.

Who is right? Is there still the possibility of accepting some kind of a compromise between these two extremes?

Next, we turn to the controversy between Calvinism and Arminianism—specifically, the contrast of the famous five points of Calvinism with the teachings of Jacob Arminius, whose theology was adopted by Charles Wesley. The debate moves on.

### Notes

1. Martin Luther, *The Bondage of the Will,* trans. Henry Cole (Grand Rapids: Baker, 1976), 36.
2. Gordon E. Rupp, ed., *Luther and Erasmus: Free Will and Salvation* (Library of Christian Classics), 8:2.
3. Erasmus, *The Diatribe* (Library of Christian Classics), 8:2.
4. Luther, 69.
5. Ibid., 69-70.
6. *Luther and Erasmus,* 57.
7. Ibid., 59.
8. Luther, 183.
9. Ibid., 73.
10. Quoted in *Christian News,* 4 Nov. 1985, 19.

# ELEVEN

# Predestination or Free Will: Calvin v. Arminius

In our generation, the names most frequently associated with the free will/predestination dispute are those of John Calvin and Jacob Arminius. As the controversy continues, it develops new twists.

John Calvin, a Frenchman, was trained in humanism but became greatly concerned about the reform of the church. Because Lutheranism was suppressed in France, Calvin fled to Geneva, Switzerland, in 1538 and was persuaded to stay there by Farel, a man who was part of the reform movement in Switzerland. There at the age of twenty-seven, Calvin published his famous *Institutes of the Christian Religion,* a clear, coherent presentation of biblical theology. For centuries to come, it served as the basic textbook of theology for much of Protestantism. Calvin's overriding concern was an understanding of the sovereignty of God and the assurance that his purposes will be accomplished.

Calvin agreed with Luther that the will of the unconverted was in bondage. Men are rescued from this slavery by God, who elects some to eternal life and others to reprobation. These doctrines are defined as "God's eternal decree by which he determined with himself what he willed to become of each man. . . . Eternal life is ordained for some; eternal damnation for others." The reason for the divine choice is inscrutable, but the choice is not arbitrary. Did God predestinate the Fall? The answer is yes; Calvin called this the dreadful decree.

In the 1600s, Calvinism met with opposition in the Netherlands. Arminius, a disciple of Beza (a follower of Calvin), became persuaded of the doctrine of free will and universal grace. He and his followers took a more moderate position regarding original sin and drafted five articles that were more in tune with Semi-Pelagianism than Calvinism. These five articles are essentially the views of evangelicalism today.

These articles were presented in a remonstrance that stirred controversy throughout Europe. Briefly they are:

1. God decreed to save all who believe and persevere in the faith; all others are left in sin and damnation.

2. Christ died for all men, "so that he has obtained for them all, by his death on the cross, redemption and forgiveness of sins; yet that no one actually enjoys this forgiveness of sins except the believer."

3. Man has not saving grace of himself, nor of the energy of his free will "inasmuch as he, in the state of apostasy and sin, can of and by himself neither think, will, or do anything that is truly good . . . but that he be born again of God in Christ."

4. Without the operation of grace, man cannot do anything good, but grace is not irresistible since men have resisted the Holy Spirit.

5. Believers partake of eternal life and have power to strive against Satan. However, whether they can fall away and be lost is a matter "that must be more particularly determined out of Holy Scripture before we ourselves can teach it with the full persuasion of our minds."

These views greatly influenced the theology of John Wesley. If God bestows prevenient grace—that is, grace that precedes human action—on all men, every sinner (though fallen) is able to believe the gospel. The depravity of man did not necessitate a belief in sovereign grace as the Calvinists had said. God gave each man enough grace to counteract the effects of depravity. Salvation was of grace, yet also dependent on the free will of man.

## The Synod of Dort
The Synod of Dort was convened in the Netherlands in 1618 to respond to the Arminian challenge. It consisted of eighty-four members and eighteen political delegates representing countries such as England, Scotland, and Switzerland. One hundred and fifty-four sessions were held with a large number of other conferences. The synod lasted from November 13, 1618, to May, 1619. During these six months, the matter of the free will of man and related doctrines was thoroughly examined. The broad representation of the council along with the carefulness of its procedure made it perhaps the most unique council in church history.

The synod strongly rejected the five articles of the Remonstrance and adopted the now famous five points of Calvinism, sometimes remembered by the acrostic TULIP—total depravity, unconditional election, limited atonement, irresistible grace, and the perseverance of the saints. The reason that only some of the race of sinful men came to faith, the synod concluded, must be attributed to the eternal council of God.

## Contrasting the Five Points
The following is a brief exposition of the five points contrasted with the five basic beliefs of Arminianism.

*1. Total Depravity.* This simply means that man inherits the guilt of Adam's sin (Rom. 5:12) and is by nature a child of wrath (Eph. 2:3). The corruption of sin extends to his

mind as well as his will; consequently, no one seeks God.
Because man is dead in trespasses and sins, God must
regenerate him and even grant him the faith to believe.

In contrast, Arminianism teaches that man is to some
degree depraved, but that he receives enough grace to
counteract the effects of depravity. The scales are therefore rather evenly balanced. So man is capable of making
his choice after all.

The Synod of Dort disagreed with the view that saving
grace is given to all men and that each must make up his
mind whether or not to receive it. True, the Bible speaks
about common grace (sunshine and rain, for example),
but saving grace is nowhere said to be given to all. Certainly the heathen who have not heard of Christ do not
have such grace. Multiplied millions of Muslims can
hardly be said to have their wills equally poised between
choosing for Christ or against him.

Arminianism said man was sick; Calvinism said man was
dead. If he is only sick, common grace might help him to
recover by enabling him to make a right choice. But if he
is spiritually dead, he needs the Giver of Life to make the
choice for him or, at least, that is what the Synod concluded.

George Whitefield described the spiritual condition of
man in terms of Lazarus, who was physically dead. The
unconverted, Whitefield said, are as bound with corrup-
tions as Lazarus was with grave clothes. They "are as
unable to raise themselves out of this loathsome dead
state as Lazarus was . . . but all their efforts, exerted with
ever so much vigor will prove quite fruitless till that same
Jesus who cried, 'Lazarus come forth' quickens them."
Indeed, Christ used this exact analogy: "For just as the
Father raises the dead and gives them life, even so the Son
also gives life to whom He wishes" (John 5:21).

Why, then, is one person saved and another lost? The
Arminian says the difference is to be found in man. On
this point, Arminianism agrees with Erasmus, who said,

that the same sun that hardens mud, softens clay. If I am saved and you are not, it is because my heart was less disposed to evil than yours.

The Calvinist says that the difference is in God, for all men are equally in bondage to sin. Any differences in disposition is due to his work in the human heart. Thus since some are saved, it must be that God has elected them. Arthur Pink, a Calvinist, said, "To say that salvation turns upon the sinner's own acceptance of Christ would be like offering a sum of money to a blind man upon the condition that he would see."[1]

Thus the doctrine of total depravity leads directly to that of unconditional election—a dead man cannot respond to the gospel's appeal.

2. Unconditional election. The synod affirmed that the reason some are saved is because God elected them to eternal life; others are condemned to eternal death. Because salvation rests wholly with God, no one can say he chose Christ because he is wiser than others; he did so because God had chosen him and quickened him that he might believe.

Calvinists have often accused the Arminians of taking at least a bit of credit for their salvation. But the Arminians did not deny that men needed the assistance of the grace of God in salvation. Recall the words of the Arminian remonstrance that man in the state of apostasy and sin "can neither think, will, nor do anything that is truly good (such as saving faith eminently is); but that it is needful that he be born again of God in Christ." What they denied was that this assistance was only granted to some and that it was irresistible.

If man makes the decision either to accept or reject Christ, what then did Paul mean when he wrote that God chose us in Christ before the foundation of the world? Arminians said that election is based on foreknowledge. Since God knows who will believe, he elects individuals only because he foresees their faith. Evidence for this is

found in such passages as 1 Peter 1:1-2, where believers
are said to be "chosen according to the foreknowledge of
God the Father." Arminians stress that God is not the one
who initiates the choice; we choose to be elected.

Calvinists point out, however, that the word *foreknowl-edge* does not just mean "to know beforehand." In both
the Old and New Testaments it means, "to regard with
favor." Amos quoted God as saying to Israel, "You only
have I chosen among all the families of the earth" (3:2).
Similarly, the New Testament uses the word in the sense of
"fore-loved." Paul wrote, "God hath not rejected His
people whom He foreknew" (Rom. 11:2). The word
cannot mean simply to know in advance but refers to
God's special favor. Other passages support this under-standing of the word (Matt. 7:23; 2 Tim. 2:19; 1 Pet. 1:20).
To be elect according to foreknowledge is to be elect on
the basis of God's favor or choice. This explains why the
word *foreknowledge* is never used with reference to
things or events but only in relation to people.

Paul wrote, "just as He chose us in Him before the
foundation of the world, that we should be holy and
blameless before Him" (Eph. 1:4). Other verses also state
that God did the choosing (2 Thess. 2:13; John 15:16).

Contemporary Arminians have suggested that election
can be based on foreknowledge because of God's perspec-tive on time. The argument is that God does not exist in
time; for him everything is one eternal *now.* Therefore,
the choice did not take place before the foundation of the
world but is actually taking place now.

The difficulty with this view is that it denies the two
truths the Scripture affirms, namely, that God did the
choosing and that the choice was made prior to creation.
Fortunately, most Arminians now admit that such explana-tions are more trouble than they are worth. And as Donald
Carson says, "They are in no sense explanatory solutions
of the sovereignty-responsibility tension. That would be
to explain the obscure by the more obscure."[2]

Obviously, we are back to the question of free will. If man's will is free, it is up to him to accept or reject Christ. On the other hand, if God made the choice, he works in the hearts of the chosen to bring them to faith. If so, man's will is not free.

Unfortunately, there is not much room for compromise. Either God chose us on his own initiative or he chose us because we chose him. Either we are dead and unable to contribute to our own resurrection or else we are only spiritually sick, able to aid our own recovery.

*3. Limited Atonement.* This means simply that Christ did not die for all men in general but gave himself only for the church, the elect. This doctrine elicits a chorus of objections from those of us who were reared in basic Arminian doctrines. At first blush, such a view seems so wrong we wonder why anyone would ever hold it. Saying "Christ died for every single individual" is the very fabric of evangelicalism.

It is important to try to understand why such an important synod would conclude that Christ died only for the elect.

Calvinists teach that this doctrine is necessary to preserve the two basic attributes of God, namely his justice and the integrity of his purposes.

The argument goes like this: Suppose I were to owe you a thousand dollars but was unable to pay my debt. But a kind friend intervenes and pays you what I owe. But you still elicit a payment from me, asking that I pay every last cent. Would that be just? I think not. If my friend paid my debt, justice requires that I be free.

The analogy is clear: if Christ's sacrifice was for all men, then either all men will be saved or God will be unfairly demanding from sinners what has already been paid. If Christ died for people who will be in hell, his justice is in jeopardy. How could a righteous God demand a double payment for the same debt?

"But," we protest, "the payment is no good unless it is

accepted." Calvinists point out that the important point is that God has *already* accepted Christ's payment on the cross. If this was a payment for the sins of the whole world, then the unbelief of the ungodly was also included in the sacrifice. No one should be expected to pay for his sin in hell. If the treachery of Judas was included in Christ's ransom, which the Father accepted, why should he be required to suffer for his sin?

Arminianism, which teaches that Christ died for all men, has sometimes led to the belief that eventually all men would be saved. This was partly behind Karl Barth's doctrine of universalism. Our responsibility, he taught, was to tell men and women that they are *already* reconciled to God. His logic was that if Christ died for all, all will be saved.

Whitefield called the doctrine of universal atonement, as taught by Arminians, blasphemy and the "highest reproach upon the dignity of the Son of God and the merit of his blood."

Spurgeon, with no less candor, argued that if Christ died to redeem all men, yet so few are saved, the death of Christ is, by and large, a failure. He wrote:

*Some persons love the doctrine of universal atonement. . . . Yet if it was Christ's intention to save every man, how deplorably has he been disappointed, for there is a lake of fire, and into that pit of woe have been cast some of the very persons who, according to the theory of universal redemption, were bought with his blood. . . . We cannot preach the gospel unless we base it upon the special and particular redemption of his elect and chosen people which Christ wrought upon the cross.*[3]

The Synod of Dort asserted that Christ actually got what he paid for. When he died, he was actually redeeming specific people—his people from their sins. He did not pay the ransom for all slaves only to bring a fraction of their number back with him. As Michael Horton put it, "Although it is absolutely essential that we trust Christ and accept his sacrifice for our sins, no one for whom Christ died will reject it. Christ's mission was accomplished!"[4]

The phrase "limited atonement" is unfortunate since it gives the impression that Christ's death was not as effective as generally believed. But actually, those who believe in this doctrine of "particular redemption" or "definite atonement" as it is better called, affirm that it is the Arminians that limit the value of the cross.

Spurgeon said Arminians assert that Christ's death did not infallibly secure the salvation of anyone. Christ could have died and yet not a single person trust him, say the Arminians. Christ's death therefore would have purchased no one. That, says Spurgeon, is limiting the value of the atonement.

Arthur Pink asked, "What exalts Christ more—an atonement which secures the salvation of everyone for whom it was made—or one which ends with the vast majority of those for whom it was made being punished in hell? What confidence can we have in a Christ who is unable to save those for whom he died?"

If it is true that Christ died to redeem a specific number of people, namely those whom the Father had given him, it follows that all believers were redeemed at the cross two thousand years ago. They were cleared of all charges then, for God accepted the ransom payment. The certificate of our canceled debt was then given to us when we trusted Christ. Paul said that the reason no one can bring a charge against the elect is that Christ has died for them (Rom. 8:24).

But does the Bible actually teach that Christ died only for the elect? Here are some of the passages used to show that Christ came for the specific purpose of paying a ransom only for those whom God had chosen:

*But He was pierced through for our* transgressions, He was crushed for *our* iniquities. (Isa. 53:5, emphasis mine)

Just as the Son of Man did not come to be served, but to serve, and to give His life a ransom for *many.* (Matt. 20:28, emphasis mine)

Be on guard for yourselves and for all the flock of God which He purchased with His own blood. (Acts 20:28)

Husbands love your wives, just as Christ also loved the church and gave Himself up *for her.* (Eph. 5:25, emphasis mine)

Husbands should be willing to die for their wives, just as Christ died for the church. Neither would die for spurious lovers. The point of all these passages is the same, namely, that Christ came not to pay a ransom for all, but to "save His people from their sins."

Arminians point to those passages that appear to teach that Christ's death was a payment for the sins of the whole world. Perhaps the clearest is 1 John 2:2, in which Christ is spoken of as the "propitiation for our sins; and not for ours only, but also for those of the whole world."

Calvinists exhort us to examine the use of the word *all* as it is used in the Bible to see if it always means each and every individual in the world. For example, when Christ said he would draw *all* men to himself, it cannot mean each person in the world—indeed the vast majority are not drawn to him but are lost. When Paul said that "as in Adam all die, so also in Christ all shall be made alive" (1 Cor. 15:22), he cannot in the second usage of the word *all* mean everyone in the world—indeed only relatively few are made alive in Christ. Such uses of the word *all* are frequent. Perhaps John meant that Christ was the propitiation for all in the world who believe, regardless of nationality or rank. Note such uses in other passages (Col. 1:6; Rom. 1:8; Luke 2:1).

Arminians (and so-called four point Calvinists) remain unconvinced. They believe that Christ suffered for all men but that the payment was only potentially made; whether or not it is received by God depends on the decision of men. Lewis Sperry Chafer pointed out that many of the elect live in open rebellion before their conversion. This proves, he says, that men are not saved simply by the fact that Christ died for them, but by the divine application of the cross when they believe. His point is that no one was *actually* redeemed at Calvary, but only *potentially* redeemed. This explains why Christ could die for all, even for those who will not believe. God accepts Christ's sacrifice piecemeal, as men believe. Thus, though all were included, the payment is applied as people respond to the message.

Five-point Calvinists demur, saying that God accepted Christ's sacrifice as a payment for sin two thousand years ago. It was not merely potentially, but *actually* accepted. "When He had made purification of sins, He sat down at the right hand of the Majesty on high" (Heb. 1:3b). Notice that purification was made at the cross; God already has received the payment for the elect.

Most Calvinists believe that Christ's death was sufficient for all; but the *intention* of the cross was to save only the elect. If God from all eternity purposed to save one portion of the human race and not another, the purpose of the cross would be to redeem these chosen ones to himself. We can know whether we belong to that number.

Did anyone hold to the doctrine of particular atonement before the Synod of Dort? Yes, there are statements that imply that this doctrine was held by men such as Justin Martyr and Cyprian. Anselm said that if you die in unbelief, Christ did not die for you. Tyndale wrote that the blood of Christ puts away only the sins of the elect.

Those interested in the topic should consult the bibliography at the end of this book for further study.

At any rate, so-called five point Calvinists and Arminians will continue to differ on such matters.

*4. Irresistible Grace.* Calvinists, in my opinion, should drop this phrase and substitute "efficacious or effectual grace." This phrase means simply that when God applies his saving grace to the elect, it is always effective. All of the elect will be saved because God's grace will accomplish God's work. As J. I. Packer wrote, "Grace proves irresistible just because it destroys the disposition to resist." As explained later, this does not mean that anyone will ever be saved against his or her will.

How do Calvinists interpret those verses that say that men have, in fact, resisted the Holy Spirit? Stephen charged the Jews with being stiffnecked and uncircumcised in heart, always resisting the Holy Spirit (Acts 7:51). Certainly, the unconverted do so. But Calvinists teach that God will of necessity give the disposition to believe to those who are chosen to eternal life. God's grace will always eventually overcome the resistance of the elect.

In contrast, Arminians believe that saving grace is given to all men and can be resisted. Here again, the difference between the two theological systems is clear.

*5. Perseverance of the Saints.* This doctrine is the logical outcome of the preceding tenets of Calvinism. Historically, it means that the saints will persevere in their faith. None of the elect will be lost. Christ affirmed, "All that the Father gives Me shall come to Me. . . . And this is the will of Him who sent Me, that of all that He has given me I lose nothing, but raise it up on the last day" (John 6:37-39).

Ironically, Arminius, the man most often associated with the view that a saved person can be lost, did not deny the perseverance of the saints. He thought, however, that the matter was open to debate. He was not as sure as the Calvinists about the matter.

Since this doctrine has many ramifications and needs more detailed exposition, an entire chapter will be devoted to it later.

Since Calvinism has played such a large role in the history of Christian doctrine, and yet is not widely accepted today, it is appropriate to clarify its teachings. Consider some of the most popular objections to the famous "five points."

## Clarifications

Calvinism has often been rejected because of some misunderstandings that have come to be associated with it. The following explanations are given not to persuade the reader to become a Calvinist but to point out how a Calvinist might reply to popular objections often leveled against this doctrine.

*Objection #1. Calvinism makes people into puppets.* God so directs the human will that we are reduced to robots. In effect, the argument goes, we are play-acting.

Is this what Calvinism teaches? The notion that God controls human beings like we might control a computer is, needless to say, contrary to the teaching of the Bible. Puppets and computers do not have wills; they cannot love or hate. They blindly follow whatever physical forces act upon them. In contrast, man has emotions, a mind that can think, and yes, a will that can make decisions. To reduce man to a puppet is to rob him of his dignity.

But what causes a man to make the decisions he does? The American theologian Jonathan Edwards said that we always choose according to the strongest inclination at the moment. We may have the desire to steal, but our fear of being caught (or the fear of the Lord) may cause us to resist that temptation. At any rate, we made our choice on the basis of the inclinations we felt. What causes a man to commit murder? He does so because he feels anger, revenge, or a sense of justice—he wants to "set the record straight."

The Calvinist does not say that God programmed the man to do evil. Calvinism does, however, teach that because of the Fall, man's desires are depraved and often exploited by Satan; therefore his inclinations are directed toward evil rather than good. So he commits a crime because he *wants* to. He does just as he desires.

For the sake of clarification, I prefer to say, with Jonathan Edwards, that fallen man acts *voluntarily* but not freely. There is a distinction. Freedom always means the ability to do the opposite—if man were really free, he could choose to live a completely righteous life on his own, or at least he could choose Christ on his own. But he cannot, so he is not free. But he does act *voluntarily,* that is, he acts according to his desires; he does whatever he wants to do. An alcoholic may not be free to quit drinking—he lacks free will with respect to this habit. Though he is not free, he does act voluntarily—he goes to the bar simply because he *wants* to. Fallen man therefore is largely self-determined; he is not forced into doing evil by external forces but does so voluntarily. James taught that the solicitation we have toward evil should not be ascribed to God. "Let no one say when he is tempted, 'I am being tempted by God'; for God cannot be tempted by evil, and He Himself does not tempt anyone" (1:13). The evil man's desires arise out of his own heart.

This is why the Westminster statement of faith can say that God ordains whatever comes to pass and yet add, "Yet so as thereby neither is God the author of sin, nor is violence done to the will of the creatures, nor is liberty or contingency of second causes taken away, but rather established." The will of man is not violated by God in the sense that God forces a man to do something he does not want to do. When the Bible says that God raises up evil men, such as Pharaoh, God may have done no more than simply withdraw any positive influence in Pharaoh's life. God's choice to do this is nevertheless the cause of Pharaoh's hard heart. After all, God could have chosen *not* to withdraw his gracious influence.

Scripture explicitly teaches that God actually ordains the evil choices of men. In the case of Judas, for example, God allowed (or used) Satan to put the idea of the betrayal in his heart. "The devil having already put into the heart of Judas Iscariot, the son of Simon to betray Him" (John 13:2). That Judas had to betray Christ is clear from repeated statements that say this happened that the Scriptures might be fulfilled. Even in such cases, however, it is reasonable to suppose that Judas had made many prior deceitful decisions so that the activity of Satan was quite compatible with his own inclinations and desires. The same applies to the many instances in the Bible in which God says the wicked do what he predetermined would happen.

Calvinism asserts that man is so fallen that he has no natural inclination to choose Christ. This desire cannot arise from man himself for no man seeks after God. A contemporary theologian, R. C. Sproul, when speaking about the natural man, says, "He lost his ability to choose Christ. In order to choose Christ, the sinner must have the desire to choose Christ. Either he has that desire already within him, or he must receive that desire from God."[5] But because he does not have that desire of himself, it must be God-given. Christ taught that no one could come to him unless the desire was given to him by his Father.

Now (and here it gets tricky) Calvinism goes on to say that God grants the inclination and ability to choose Christ to some, namely, the elect. God does not *coerce* anyone, if that means he saves a man against his will.

We may choose to give a thief money, not because we *want* to but because we have a gun pointed at our head (that is coercion). Needless to say, God does not coerce a person to believe. There is no such thing as a person who doesn't want to be saved and God saves him anyway because he is elect. Nor has any person ever existed who would like to be saved but cannot be because he is not elect. God works in the lives of those who are to be saved, convicting them of sin and giving them the faith to believe the gospel. *He changes their disposition so they get saved because they want to.*

Christ taught, "All that the Father gives me shall come to

me; and the one who comes I will certainly not cast out" (John 6:37). All that the Father gives shall come, and when they do they will be received. God works in the hearts of the elect so that they desire to come to Christ. When D. L. Moody quipped, "The elect are the whosoever wills and the nonelect are the whosoever won'ts," he was right. Calvinists could not agree more.

Does this mean that God has violated man's freedom? Again, I must stress that fallen man's freedom is one-sided, that is, he is free only to choose various shades of evil. Even the good he does is tainted, so that God cannot accept it. So the freedom he has is quite limited.

Furthermore, none of us chose whether or not we would be born, nor did we choose our parents or place of our birth. Since these matters were determined by God, does he not also have the right to change the desires of the human heart so that man will choose to believe on his son?

No believer is inclined to object to the fact that God has worked in his or her heart to bring about salvation. Those who disdain the belief that God brings those whom he has chosen to repentance should remember that if left to our "free will," we would all be lost.

If you were drowning and unconscious in the water, you would be quite pleased if the lifeguard rescued you even though he (and not you) made the decision that you be rescued. Of course in salvation (unlike a man drowning) our wills are involved. But the point to be made is that Calvinism says we responded because God has inclined our will that we choose him.

To summarize, both Arminians and Calvinists agree that God must work in the human heart if one is to be saved. They differ sharply, however, over the extent of the involvement that God has in decisions that affect salvation. The difference is this: Arminians believe that God can only "woo" or "plead," but he can never work in the human will in such a way as to render the decision certain.

Calvinists insist that there are at least some decisions that are made certain because of God's purposes. For example, no man chosen by God for salvation can fail to come to Christ. Again I quote John 6:37, "*All* that the Father gives Me shall come to Me" (emphasis mine).

I must point out that Arminians who stress the freedom of the will nevertheless pray that the unconverted might come to Christ. Is not this a tacit admission that God has the ability to work in the human will to bring about salvation? If God does not "tamper with the human will" (as one Arminian puts it), why bother to pray that the unsaved will be drawn to the Savior?

The strength of Arminianism is that it makes a sincere attempt to preserve free will by making salvation dependent on man's choice and not God's. Calvinism's strength is that it makes the intention of God to save a given number certain. It insists that all men are spiritually dead, so if some are quickened, it must be because of a difference in God, not man.

We must have the humility to admit that we may never know what part God, man, and the devil play in any specific decision made by us humans. The relationship between these three personalities may vary in different situations. Calvinism says that God works in the human heart either directly or indirectly to accomplish his purposes and so that the outcome of at least some decisions is rendered certain by his decree.

*Objection #2. How can man be held accountable for his actions if he does not have free will?* Is God fair in calling fallen men into account whose nature is depraved? For a sinful man to sin is only to act according to nature.

Jonathan Edwards tried to answer this objection by distinguishing between "natural ability" and "moral ability." Man has the natural ability to make righteous decisions because he has a mind, moral consciousness, and will. What he lacks is *moral* ability because his disposition is evil.

Edwards would agree that it would be unjust for God to expect an elephant to fly since the beast does not have wings. But man has the wings (that is the equipment to make right decisions) but lacks the disposition to use that equipment rightly.

Pelagius, you will recall, taught that whatever man should do, he could do. Paul, however, taught that he could not do what he should: "For that which I am doing, I do not understand; for I am not practicing what I would like to do, but I am doing the very thing I hate" (Rom. 7:15). Luther said that only when men realize that God even holds them accountable for what they cannot do are they inclined to cast themselves on the mercy of God.

Also, as argued above, Calvinism teaches that men make choices according to their own desires. They are not "determined" by God like a puppet on a string. Men do what they want to do and are held accountable. True, there is much that they *cannot* do—righteousness, for example. But they are responsible for what they *do* do.

Suppose you were born into a family that was greatly in debt. The responsibility for payment would fall on you, even if the debt was incurred before your time. So we inherit the sin of our forefather Adam, and God holds us accountable for it. Not only are we born with a sin nature, but we are also under condemnation. We are therefore held accountable for sins we did not personally commit.

If you object to this, remember that Arminianism does not escape this difficulty either. Both Arminians and Calvinists admit that millions of people will be lost even though they had no choice whatever to believe on Christ. God will judge these people on the basis of their knowledge, even though they knew nothing about the gospel. Responsibility, Arminians must admit, is based on the degree of knowledge a person has, not on whether or not he has a genuine option to accept or reject Christ.

*Problem #3. Calvinism makes God inconsistent.* He offers the gospel to all men, yet all cannot believe. Luther, you will recall, appealed to a "hidden will of God" that was distinct from the revealed will of God. The revealed will was that all men be saved, but the hidden will was that the greater part of mankind be dammed. Arminians say that this not only sets up a conflict in the nature of God but gives reason to believe that God is deceitful. He offers with one hand what he takes away with another. What about the existence of a hidden purpose or will that is contrary to the revealed will of God? To put it differently, does God ever give an invitation to men that he knows they cannot accept?

He did so to Pharaoh. Read carefully, "And the Lord said unto Moses, 'When you go back to Egypt see that you perform before Pharaoh all the wonders which I have put in your power; but I will harden his heart so that he will not let the people go' " (Exod. 4:21).

The revealed will of God was that the Lord wanted Pharaoh to let the people go; the hidden purpose was that Pharaoh's heart would be hardened so that he would not let the people go. God told Moses to make a request of Pharaoh that he knew the king could not possibly accept. Indeed, God himself made sure Pharaoh could not accept it.

Was God insincere in his offer to Pharaoh? Was he taking away with one hand what he was offering with another? Were these two revelations of God in conflict with one another?

There are other examples. Ezekiel was sent to speak to the house of Israel even though God told him in advance that the people would not hear (Ezek. 3:4-11).

Isaiah was told to speak to the people of his day though God said that the people's hearts would be hardened (Isa. 6:9-11). Christ said that the people were being sent prophets and wise men even though they would not be received (Matt. 23:34-36).

Calvinists maintain that there is nothing deceitful about God making an offer to men and women that he knows they will refuse or even an offer he knows they cannot accept. It would be deceitful if the offer were accepted and then God did not meet his promised obligations. God may be using this universal offer as a future basis of judgment, as in the instances cited from Scripture.

Actually, this objection to Calvinism applies to Arminianism, too. If God knows who will be saved and who will not (as Arminians admit), then is not God insincere in offering salvation to those whom he knows will not accept it? And if, indeed, God knows they will not accept it, is not this in effect the same as saying they *cannot* accept it? After all, God's foreknowledge is not faulty. To put it clearly, if God knows they will not accept his offer they *cannot* accept it, regardless of the reason why they say no.

*Objection #4. How can we harmonize "God elected some" with "God desires all to be saved"?* Paul wrote that God "desires all men to be saved and to come to the knowledge of the truth" (1 Tim. 2:4), and again it is said that he is patient, "not wishing for any to perish but for all to come to repentance" (2 Pet. 3:9).

The word *will* is often used in Scripture in the sense of *desire.* In this context the idea is that God does not desire that men and women be lost in perdition. This is consistent with the Old Testament assertion that God does not delight in the death of the wicked.

But there is a difference between the *decree* of God and the *desire* of God. A moment's reflection will confirm this distinction. Think of it this way: God did not delight in the death of his Son. We could say that he was not willing that his Son die and suffer in agony upon the cross. Yet, he decreed that it would happen. Christ died at the hands of wicked men doing whatsoever God's hand "predestined to occur" (Acts 4:28). Clearly, God chose to forego his desires. He desired one thing but decreed another. If we ask why, all that we can do is reply that he had an overriding purpose to accomplish. That purpose overshadowed his desire to see Christ exempt from suffering.

Similarly, he *desires* that all men be saved. Yet, on the other hand, he allows the greater part of humanity to perish. We simply do not know why he has chosen to forgo his desire to see all men be saved. We can be quite sure, however, that there is some ultimate purpose, for the Scripture says, "The Lord has made everything for its own purpose, even the wicked for the day of evil" (Prov. 16:4).

*Problem #5. Why didn't God elect all?* Calvinists must explain why God did not elect all (or at least more) to eternal life if it was within his power to do so.

Behind this objection is the assumption that God owes salvation to everyone. But the Calvinist believes that God was not obligated to save anybody. If he saves some, that does not put him under obligation to save the rest. If we got what we deserved, we would all be lost.

As R. C. Sproul points out, God does not treat everyone equally. God did not appear to Hammurabi in the same way as he appeared to Moses; God gave blessings to Israel he did not give to Persia. Christ appeared to Paul on the way to Damascus in a way that he did not appear to Pilate. Then he adds, "In the plan of salvation God does nothing bad. He never commits an injustice. Some people get justice, which is what they deserve, while others get mercy."[6]

Warfield points out that the love of God must of necessity be under the control of God's righteousness and his eternal purposes. In answer to the question as to why God doesn't save more people, Warfield said that the old answer is still the best one: "God in his love saves as many of the guilty race of man as he can get the consent of his whole nature to save." He cannot exercise his raw power to save without taking his other attributes and his eternal objectives into account.

In the next chapter we shall see that Arminianism does not really explain why so few are saved. Both systems must accept the fact that only a fraction of the world's

population is coming to know Christ as Savior. Both
believe that God could have arranged the salvation of
many more if that were his only priority. More of that later.

I cannot emphasize enough that Calvinists agree with
Arminians that whoever desires to be saved can be. We
can know whether our names were written in the Book of
Life from before the foundation of the world (Rev. 13:8).
We must come to Christ, and his promise is that he will
not cast us out (John 6:37).

## Contrasting the Views

J. I. Packer is a Calvinist whose introduction to John
Owen's book, *The Death of Death in the Death of Christ,*
gives a clear contrast between Arminianism and Calvinism.
Admittedly it is biased, for Packer argues that Calvinism
alone gives the correct understanding of salvation.

He sees Arminianism as teaching that God is waiting in
"quiet impotence" at the door of our hearts, waiting for us
to let him in. He continues, "We have flattered impenitent
sinners by assuring them that it is in their power to repent
and believe, though God cannot make them do it." For
Arminianism teaches that after God and Christ have done
all they can or will, it depends finally on each man's
choice whether God's purpose to save men is to be
realized or not. Salvation is out of God's hands and placed
into the hands of men.

Packer urged us to preach a gospel that overthrows
self-confidence "to convince sinners that salvation is
altogether out of their hands, and to shut them up to a
self-despairing dependence on the glorious grace of a
sovereign Savior, not only for their righteousness but for
their faith too."[7] This, of course, is Calvinism.

But Calvinism is not easy for any of us to accept. John Wesley
believed it made God a devil, or rather, worse than the devil.
He and Whitefield, though initially friends, split over this
doctrine. Let's take one more look at this critical debate.

## Notes

1. Arthur Pink, *The Atonement* (Sterling, Va.: Reiner Publications, 1971), 245.
2. Donald A. Carson, *Divine Sovereignty and Human Responsibility* (Atlanta: John Knox Press, 1981), 210.
3. Quoted in Michael Scott Horton, *Mission Accomplished* (Nashville: Nelson, 1986), 173. A similar statement occurs in Spurgeon's sermon on Isaiah 53:10, *A Treasury of the Old Testament* (Grand Rapids: Zondervan, 1962), 3:751.
4. Horton, 89.
5. R. C. Sproul, *Chosen by God* (Wheaton, Ill.: Tyndale House, 1986), 61.
6. Ibid., 37.
7. J. I. Packer in John Owen, *The Death of Death in the Death of Christ* (London: The Banner of Truth Trust, 1959), 1-25.

# TWELVE

# Predestination or Free Will: Whitefield v. Wesley

George Whitefield is by any standard one of the greatest preachers of all time. When he was but twenty-two years old, revivals sprung up in and around London as a result of his preaching. During this time, John and Charles Wesley were attempting to do missionary work in Georgia but were failing badly. A few months after their return to England, John Wesley was converted at Aldersgate where he heard the reading of Martin Luther's preface to his commentary on Romans. Even after that he continued to suffer doctrinal and spiritual uncertainty.

Meanwhile, Whitefield's ministry was so remarkable that it was reported, "All London and the whole nation ring of the great things of God done by his ministry." Because he knew Wesley from their days at Oxford, he invited him to join him in preaching to the large crowds. Whitefield often referred to himself as a Methodist, so he was thought of as the founder of Methodism. Wesley's crowds were not as big as Whitefield's at this time, but he was beginning to achieve a measure of fame.

When Whitefield introduced him to his congregation at Bristol, he urged him to enter no dispute, "least of all, concerning predestination because the people were so prejudiced for it." But Wesley began to preach against predestination, a doctrine that Whitefield was becoming convinced was true.

When Whitefield sailed for America in 1739, he entrusted his large congregation to Wesley. He had no thought that Wesley would use the occasion to turn the people against him over the two matters of predestination and perfectionism. Yet, now Wesley began to preach against what Whitefield taught. He who abhorred Calvinism now became the leader of a revival movement that had been started by Whitefield, the Calvinist.[1]

Shortly after Whitefield sailed for America, Wesley preached his sermon on free grace. He also put a copy into the hands of printers in America and thereby Whitefield learned of the sermon. When Whitefield returned from America, he discovered that Wesley had turned the people against him. Wesley had asked that the people not come within earshot of Whitefield. And after Whitefield continued his ministry, Wesley followed him around to sow division over the matter of election. One day, Charles Wesley asked his brother to come with him, but John replied, "It is not possible for me to set out yet. I must go around and glean after G. Whitefield."

What was the content of that sermon, "Free Grace," that made the breach between Wesley and Whitefield irreparable?

Wesley made the point that Calvinism teaches that by the decree of God, the greater part of humanity abides in death without any possibility of redemption; no one can save this vast multitude except God, and he will not save them. "To say that God hath decreed not to save them is the same as saying that he hath decreed to damn them. Call it whatever name you please, election, preterition, predestination or reprobation . . . it comes in the end to the same thing. . . . By virtue of an eternal, unchangeable decree of God, one part of mankind is infallibly saved, and the rest infallibly damned."

He then concluded that this would make all preaching vain. "It is needless to them that are elected . . . it is useless to them that are not." In effect, it makes preaching the gospel unnecessary.

Wesley called predestination a doctrine "full of blasphemy." It represents our blessed Lord as "a hypocrite, a deceiver of the people, a man void of common sincerity. Such blasphemy . . . as might make the ears of a Christian tingle." Addressing Whitefield, he said, "You represent God as worse than the devil; as more false, more cruel, and more unjust. . . . You say you will prove it with the Scripture! Hold! What will you prove by Scripture? that God is worse than the devil? It cannot be."

Wesley still wasn't finished. He then turned to address the devil:

*Thou fool, why dost thou roar about any longer? Thy lying in wait for souls is as needless and useless as our preaching. Hearest thou not, that God hath taken thy work out of thy hands; and that he doeth it more effectually? . . . We may resist thee; but he can irresistibly destroy both soul and body in hell! Thou canst only entice; but his unchangeable decree to leave thousands of souls in death compels them to continue in sin till they drop into everlasting burnings. . . . Hearest thou not that God is the devouring lion, the destroyer of souls, the murderer of men?*[2]

Perhaps no more scathing denunciation of Calvinism has ever been written. It seemed so plain to Wesley that Arminianism was correct that he gave very little scriptural support for his views. He appealed to the fact that the gospel is offered to all men, and that for him was enough proof that man, not God, makes the choice as to who will be saved.

But if Augustine, Luther, Calvin, Whitefield, and Jonathan Edwards were actually teaching blasphemy, how

could they have been led astray? These men were careful
students of the Scriptures. Had they missed something? To
make God the devil is a serious charge indeed. Perhaps
we need to look once more at what Calvinism teaches and
why.

Before summarizing some of the issues involved, let us
consider the Calvinist-Arminian dispute in America.

## The Decline of Calvinism in America

The Puritans who had such a great impact on the religious
life in the colonies were, for the most part, Calvinists who
believed in predestination and the bondage of the will.
The first Great Awakening ( 1740–1760 ) was largely
Calvinistic, stressing God's sovereignty in the salvation of
sinners. Most people know something of the impact of
Jonathan Edwards and his stress on the wrath of God. His
most scholarly work, entitled *The Freedom of the Will,*
classifies him among the greatest theologians of America.
In this book, which he had thought about for several years
but wrote in about five months, he argued cogently that
Arminianism was logically impossible. The will, he argued,
was not free.

But by the second Great Awakening ( 1790–1840 ),
Calvinism had declined, particularly because of the influence of the revivalist Charles Finney, who was much
closer to Pelagius than to Augustine or Calvin. He also
introduced "altar calls" into American evangelicalism.
Since that time, American theology has not been the same.

Dr. Oliver Wendell Holmes, of the Supreme Court, is
known for introducing moral relativism into the interpretation of the Constitution. He is also known for teaching
that Calvinism officially died in the United States on
November 1, 1855. He rebelled against the Calvinism of
his father, the pastor of the First Congregational Church in
Cambridge, Massachusetts. So he wrote the epitaph of
Calvinism, a poem entitled "The Wonderful 'One-Hoss

Shay,' " that signified the disintegration of this theological system. Like a one-horse chariot, Calvinism collapsed.[3]

*Have you heard of the wonderful one-hoss shay,*
*That was built in such a logical way*
*It ran a hundred years to a day,*
*And then, of a sudden, it-ah, but stay*
*I'll tell you what happened without delay,*
*Scaring the parson into fits,*
*Frightening people out of their wits—*
*Have you ever heard of that, I say?*

The poem goes on to tell how the one-hoss shay was built one hundred years ago, and then it suddenly collapsed:

*All at once, and nothing first—*
*Just as bubbles do when they burst.*
*End of the wonderful one-hoss shay.*
*Logic is logic. That's all I say.*

If Calvinism died on November 1, 1855, it was, to a large degree, due to Finney's revivalism. In reacting to the Calvinism of his day, Finney minimized the need for the grace of God in salvation. For him, man had the power to determine his own destiny; indeed, he believed that the Millennium was just around the corner. Men could have a revival whenever they wanted one. "A revival is not a miracle or dependent on a miracle. It is purely the right use of constituted means."

Finney, like Pelagius, believed that whatever a man was commanded to do, he could do. He preached a controversial sermon entitled "Sinners Bound to Change Their Own Hearts," in which he affirmed that man was not as depraved as the Calvinists had believed. Human nature was not irredeemably bad but capable of improvement. When sin begins in a child, it "is entirely the result of temptation to selfishness arising out of the circumstances under

which the child comes to being." If we could just remove
the temptations, human nature could be bettered.

Finney's Arminianism went so far as to assert that God
could not have prevented the coming of sin into the
world. Sinners could thwart the power of God by hardening their own hearts against the work of the Spirit. He
complained that Calvinists were inconsistent in that they
preached sinners should repent; yet in the same message
he would tell them that they were incapable of doing so.
To say that sinners could not repent was to slander God
with infinite tyranny.

For the most part, evangelicalism today stands with
Finney rather than Whitefield and Edwards. Most of us
were taught that Satan casts a vote against our salvation;
God casts a vote in favor, and we break the tie. Because of
the widespread belief that God does not interfere with
our "free will," one well-known evangelist told his audi-
ence, "You must make your decision alone; not even God
can make it for you. It's all up to you."

To believe in the freedom of the will is more to our
liking than is the bondage of the will, as taught by Augustine, Luther, Calvin, Edwards, and Whitefield. If Arminianism can give a satisfying answer to how God relates
to man, and if it can be shown that the Bible teaches free
will, then it appears to be preferable to Calvinism. No one
wants to make God out to be worse than the devil.

Why is Arminianism more appealing? First, it seems to
give a more acceptable answer to the problem of evil.
Calvinists say that God *ordains* evil, whereas Arminians
say that God merely permits it to happen. This seems to
protect the reputation of God.

Second, Arminianism seems to be more compatible
with the love of God. The picture of a God who is saving
as many people as he can without violating the human
will is consistent with love, whereas the idea that God
predestinated only a few to eternal life is not.

Finally, Arminians say that the Bible teaches freedom of

the will. God works in the human heart, pleading with men that they might be saved, but he never determines their decision. This is what gives impetus to the Great Commission.

Let's examine these claims.

## The Advantages of Arminianism

Wesley and Whitefield, despite their sharp differences on the doctrine of predestination, were both mightily used of God. Before his death, Whitefield graciously asked Wesley to preach his funeral sermon as a sign of unity among believers. Wesley accepted the invitation and at the funeral gave Whitefield an outstanding tribute. He characterized him as one who had unparalleled zeal, tenderheartedness, and charity. And what was the foundation of his integrity, sincerity, courage, and patience and every other valuable quality? Wesley said, "It was no other than faith in a bleeding Lord; faith in the operation of God. . . . It was the love of God shed abroad in his heart by the Holy Ghost, which was given to him, filling his soul with tender, disinterested love to every child of man."[4]

Wesley hoped that the hostility between the two theological camps would end. This, of course, is an important lesson for us as well. The body of Christ is already divided over many issues that weaken our witness to the world. Though both Arminians and Calvinists believe strongly that their respective positions are correct and important to evangelism and discipleship, both groups are used of God.

Arminians often wonder why anyone would be a Calvinist. Calvinists, in turn wonder how anyone could be an Arminian. In the pages that follow, we will consider the advantages of Arminianism and give a Calvinistic critique, not to persuade the reader to become a Calvinist, but to briefly explain why Calvinists believe that Arminianism, despite its initial attractiveness, faces biblical and logical difficulties. Since Calvinism has played such a major role in the history of Europe and America, it is important that we understand it, even if it is unpopular in our pulpits. What are the advantages of Arminianism?

*Advantage #1. God never ordains evil* but only permits it because of the free will of his creatures. In contrast, Calvinism, in saying that God actually ordains evil, makes God out to be a being who wills the suffering of man. Arminianism protects the reputation of God; Calvinism does not.

Clark Pinnock, a contemporary Arminian, says that Calvinism makes "God some kind of a terrorist who goes around handing out torture or disaster and even is willing people to do things the Bible says God hates."[5] He then refers to a madman who killed twenty people in a McDonald's restaurant as an example of the kind of atrocities Calvinists say God ordained. What Pinnock appears to believe is that these incidents happen because God does not interfere with a person's free will. So God "permits" such crimes, but they are in no way ordained. Thus, the reputation of God is preserved.

Calvinists are not convinced. Even if we grant men all the free will Pinnock desires, God could have prevented this incident. The madman could have died in his sleep during the night or at least he could have awakened too sick to get out of bed; his gun could have jammed. Or he could have been protected from the power of Satan, who most likely inspired the awful deed. Most Arminians would agree that there were all kinds of options available to God to prevent this crime, even without jeopardizing the man's free will.

If God does not will human suffering, what shall we say of the earthquake in Mexico that killed not twenty, but nearly twenty thousand? The personal grief of the city was beyond comprehension. Here is a tragedy that did not involve anyone's free will but was caused by a fault in the earth. God could have prevented the earth from shifting without compromising the freedom that the Arminians tell us we all have. God could have strengthened the earth beneath Mexico City as he has done in those parts of the world that seldom, if ever, experience earthquakes. To the terrified populace, it is a small comfort to be told that God didn't ordain it but only chose to permit it.

Suppose I am a mechanic standing beside a man who while fixing a flat tire has the car fall on him. Though the jack had held for several minutes, it gave way just as he decided to crawl under to wipe a drop of oil from the transmission. I stand by, watching the man die, though I have a hoist attached to my truck. I justify my inactivity by saying that I didn't ordain that the man die; I just permitted it. In fact, he went under the car by his own free will. Does that absolve me of responsibility? Hardly.

Now think of God: He created the man, knows the precise weight of the car and its center of gravity. He created the rock that caused the flat in the first place. He was on hand when the jack was formed and knew the strength of the metal. He could have easily arranged that the jack hold the car thirty seconds longer. But he permitted it to give way at the precise moment the man was underneath. Does it really help to say that he didn't ordain it, that he only permitted it? If a human being cannot avoid responsibility by saying he only permitted the man to die, how much less can a sovereign God avoid responsibility by saying he only permitted the accident to happen!

Calvinists think that Arminianism does not resolve the problem of evil after all. In fact, it only calls God's power into question. Was he actually helpless when a man shot twenty others? Did he overlook the weakness of the earth's crust in Mexico? Did he underestimate the weight of the car in relationship to the jack? How many things are there that happen in this sinful world without his permission and control?

Both Calvinists and Arminians teach that God does not and cannot *do* evil. Calvinists say that God nonetheless

ordains it through secondary causes. Arminians say God
only permits it. Nonetheless, his permission necessarily
means that he bore ultimate responsibility for it. After all,
he could have chosen "not to permit" it.

The Bible nowhere attempts to defend God's reputation
as we are often inclined to do. When God wanted to
punish Israel by using the armies of a wicked power, he
did not evade responsibility by distinguishing between
what he permits and what he ordains. He pointedly said,
" 'For behold, I am raising up the Chaldeans, that fierce
and impetuous people who march throughout the earth
to seize dwelling places which are not theirs' " (Hab. 1:6).
And again, God speaks, "If a calamity occurs in a city has
not the Lord done it?" (Amos 3:6). Dozens of similar
verses occur in both the Old and New Testaments.

The problem of God's relationship to evil is notoriously
difficult. Without question, it is the most baffling issue we
could ever confront. This brief discussion is not intended
to explain the ramifications of the problem, much less
solve it. My point is to show that when Arminians say that
God only permits evil but doesn't ordain it, they cannot
thereby absolve God of responsibility for evil in the
world. Calvinists pointedly admit that God ordains evil—
this is consistent with both the Bible and logic.

In ordinary discussions about human events, we can say
that God permitted evil, as long as we understand that he
thereby *willed* that the evil happen. Calvinists agree with
the Westminster Confession of Faith that says God ordains
*all* that ever comes to pass. In a word, what God permits,
he ordains.

Arminians can, of course, exercise their free will and
disagree!

*Advantage #2. God saves all he can.* The Arminian
belief that God is saving as many people as he can and
would save more if he could is more consistent with the
love of God than the view that he elected only a few to
eternal life.

Arminianism says that God gave man free will; though God may plead with men and women to repent, he never works in their hearts in such a way as actually to determine their decision. So he does his best to save as many as he can, but his respect for human freedom means that his options are limited.

Norman Geisler, defending Arminianism, writes, "Indeed, God would save all people if he could. . . . God will achieve the greatest number he possibly can. . . . God will save the greatest number actually achievable without violating their free choice."[6]

So God is doing his best. Mission leaders tell us that although multitudes are coming to Christ, the church is not keeping up with the population on a percentage basis. There are twelve countries in which there is no known indigenous church; ten of these are Muslim nations. Even in a country like the United States, where the gospel is preached from coast to coast, the number of born-again believers is relatively small. Statistically, God is losing.

There is, of course, nothing inconsistent with saying that God sovereignly chose to give man free will, and, therefore, God can only beg and plead, hoping that more would believe. If, as Geisler says, God is saving as many as he can but is encountering too much resistance, so be it. Calvinists say, however, that this is not what the Bible teaches nor is it consistent with other options that are open to him.

If it is true that God gives the ability to believe to all people by giving them enough grace to counter the effects of depravity, if the human will is as free as the Armininans say it is, we would expect that approximately half of all those who hear the gospel would receive Christ as Savior. Remember, Arminians say that each man has the free will to believe. Surprisingly, most of them exercise free will in the wrong direction.

Even if the fault lies with the church, the fact is that God has often "permitted" hindrances to the gospel to occur. Hundreds of missionaries have died at early ages because of disease or untimely deaths. A missionary pilot was killed in his first flight in India; four young missionaries died of tuberculosis just before they were to sail to Africa. If God's overriding priority is saving as many as possible, such setbacks to his cause need not have happened. These obstacles could be easily overcome without infringing on anyone's free will.

Even beyond this, God has a number of options open to him to prevent people from going into eternal perdition. Since God foreknows who will believe and who will not, he could arrange that those who will not believe die in infancy and go to heaven. Or better, why even bother to create those whom he foreknew would end in perdition? Christ said of Judas, "It were good for that man if he had not been born." God could easily have arranged that it be so. Judas would not have had to be in eternal torment.

Arminians must explain why God's goal of saving as many as he can seems to be failing. He is actively working to save as many as he can, but only a small percentage of the population is willing to believe.

One Arminian, determined to defend God against the charge of failure, suggested that in the end there will be more saved than lost because of the high infant mortality rate in underdeveloped countries. God allows mass starvation and disease so that millions of babies die and go to heaven. In this way he can save more than if he allows them to grow up and be spiritually lost.

Aside from these doubtful statistics, it is not a credit to the Almighty to say that he must resort to the starvation of infants in order to increase the number of the saved. Clark Pinnock defends God's inability to save the world by saying that creating free creatures was "risky business." He writes, "I can only suppose that he believed it was a risk worth taking in view of the benefits that would accrue."[7]

Arminians teach that God is frustrated by the free will

of his creatures. He decrees to save as many as possible, but the numbers are comparatively few. He plans and wills the salvation of all, but his goals remain unfulfilled. In fact, since God granted man free will, it is theoretically possible that no one would have even been saved.

Calvinists believe that election makes the success of God's plan certain. God has committed himself to save a certain number, and they will be saved, despite the rebellion of mankind. The unbelief and failure of man can never thwart the intended plan of God.

When the Christians in Rome thought that the purposes of God were failing because the nation Israel was not turning to Christ, Paul faced their doubt directly by saying, "But it is not as though the word of God has failed" (Rom. 9:6). Then he launched into a discussion about the sovereign purposes of God, saying in effect, it never was God's intention to save all the Israelites but only a remnant. *Since all the elect are being saved, God's purposes are being fully realized.*

He picked up the same theme in Romans 11, asserting, "In the same way then, there has also come to be at the present time a remnant according to God's gracious choice. . . . What then? That which Israel is seeking for, it has not obtained, but those who were chosen obtained it, and the rest were hardened" (Rom. 11:5-7). Those whom God intended to save are saved.

As might be expected, Arminians teach that God's choices in Romans 9 have nothing to do with personal salvation, only earthly temporal blessings. God chose Israel as a special nation, but within this group, it was up to each individual as to whether or not he would be saved. This view is difficult to substantiate from the context.

But regardless of how one interprets Romans 9, one fact is inescapable, namely, that God makes choices that in turn determine the choices men make (even if the choices are interpreted as merely earthly and temporal). God is not just pleading and wooing in this chapter but making sovereign choices that affect the human will. The hardening of Pharaoh's heart is but one example.

As Paul moved through the passage, he knew that the natural response of the readers would be, "You will say to me then, 'Why does He still find fault? For who resists His will?' " (v. 19). If Arminianism were correct, we would expect Paul to answer, "God finds fault because men have a free will and therefore could have chosen to be obedient." Here is his opportunity to set the record straight. But Paul said nothing about free will. Rather, he said, "On the contrary, who are you, O man, who answers back to God? The thing molded will not say to the molder, 'Why did you make me like this,' will it?" (v. 20). The potter has power over the clay to make one vessel unto honor and another to dishonor. God's purposes in salvation history are being fulfilled.

For the person who believes God is failing, Christ said, "All that the Father gives Me shall come to me, and the one who comes to Me I will certainly not cast out" (John 6:37). As Carson said, "The context demands that Jesus is repudiating any idea that the Father has sent the Son forth on a mission which could fail because of the unbelief of the people."[8]

Contrary to Pinnock, there is no risk in God's purposes. God is not losing the battle against the devil, even though many are on the broad road that leads to destruction and few are on the narrow way that leads to life. *All* that the Father has given Christ will come to him.

If God is interested in preserving free will, Arminians must explain why he allows Satan to blind "the minds of the unbelieving, that they might not see the light of the gospel of the glory of Christ, who is the image of God" (2 Cor. 4:4). Satan, Jesus taught, takes the Word out of the minds of men.

Why was Satan allowed in the Garden of Eden? God gave clear instructions to Adam and Eve. Why were they not permitted to make up their own minds without an alien, seductive influence? Satan could have been confined to another planet. Even today, the human mind could be placed off limits for his activity. Instead, we read that we should admonish those who are deceived, "if perhaps God may grant them repentance . . . and they may come to their senses and escape from the snare of the devil, having been held captive by him to do his will" (2 Tim. 2:26). Think of how many more would be saved if Satan were not allowed to work in their hearts. Man would have more freedom, not less.

Calvinists agree that if God is saving as many as he can but cannot save more because of the hardness of the human heart, this seems to be more consistent with the love of God. But they believe that we must define God's love in accordance with the total teaching of Scripture, which includes the doctrine of election and God's ultimate purpose for mankind.

*Advantage #3. Arminianism fosters evangelism; Calvinism leads to fatalism.* We have all heard someone say, "If a certain number are elect and they will be saved, why should we bother to witness? Whatever will be, will be."

There is no doubt that some Christians have used Calvinism as an excuse for their lack of missionary zeal, a serious charge, since the Bible is so clear about our need to evangelize and participate in the Great Commission. Perhaps here, at last, Arminianism has a tactical advantage. If the choice as to who will be saved depends on man, not God, the urgency of the gospel appeal can be maintained.

But wait! Classical Armininism believes that God actually knows who will believe and who will not, and this number can neither be increased or diminished since God's knowledge cannot be faulty. Therefore, even if we say that man makes the choice, the end result must still be considered as fixed.

Clark Pinnock, who thinks that God took a risk when he

chose to create the world, believes that God does not know the decisions of men in advance. He writes that genuine novelty "can appear in history which cannot even be predicted by God."[9] For Pinnock, election cannot even be on the basis of foreknowledge. Not even God knows who the elect are until they believe!

Even most Arminians agree that such a view is not worthy of refutation. But we must ask why Pinnock would break with classical Arminianism and actually assert that God himself does not know in advance whether or not a man will accept Christ or reject him. Pinnock believes (quite rightly) that if God knows the future with accuracy, then the number of the saved is already certain, even on Arminian premises. Therefore to have genuine freedom, Pinnock thinks, one must say that not even God knows what men will decide until they actually make a choice. So Pinnock takes the view that God cannot even predict the future accurately.

Pinnock keenly feels the force of the argument that if God foresees who will believe, then the number of those who will be saved is fixed. Even if, as Arminians believe, foreknowledge does not *cause* anything to happen, still the future will unfold as God knows it will. Yes, even for Arminians, whatever will be, will be.

The truth is that neither the Calvinist nor the Arminian has a satisfying answer to this dilemma. The most that either can say is that God uses *means* to bring about certain *ends;* therefore, we can be meaningfully involved in the evangelization of the world.

An illustration may help. We all agree that God knows the exact day we are going to die. But this doesn't mean that we drive through red lights, jump off buildings, or have arsenic for supper. God uses our common sense to keep us alive until the day he knows we will die! In just this way he uses us to bring the gospel to the elect. Spurgeon said that the doctrine of election gave him confidence when he preached, knowing that if God had not chosen some, none would be converted.

Whitefield pointed out that God's declaration to Noah that seed time and harvest would not cease does not mean that man should neglect plowing, nor does it render the heat of the sun unnecessary. To the one who is troubled about his final destiny, Whitefield asked why should such a one not strive, "since he knows not but what this striving may bring him to a state of grace."

God's choice of those who will be saved appears to be neither random nor arbitrary. He planned the *context* in which they would be converted. That is why I have never wondered whether my children are among the elect. Since they were born into a Christian home, we can believe that the means of their salvation will be the faithful teaching of God's Word. God's decision to save us involved planning where we would be born and the circumstances that would lead us to Christ. Election is part of a total picture.

Men such as Whitefield and Jonathan Edwards wept as they admonished men and women to repent. They believed that God had not only planned the end (who would be saved) but also the means by which it would happen (the prayers and witness of godly men and women sharing the gospel in power).

The fact that someone is elect does not mean that they are yet saved. Though redeemed on Calvary, they have to come to the point of personal faith in Christ. That is why Paul said, "For this reason I endure all things for the sake of those who are chosen, that they also may obtain the salvation which is in Christ Jesus and with it eternal glory" (2 Tim. 2:10). So we endure for the sake of the elect.

And, of course, as mentioned elsewhere, anyone who desires to put faith in Christ may do so. The desire and ability is a gift of God given to the elect.

## What Does the Bible Teach?

The final arbiter in the dispute is the Bible. Does it teach free will? Is it true that God coaxes and pleads but never makes the decision as to what man will do? Remember that both classical Arminianism and Calvinism teach that God influences the human will. The dispute is over the extent of that influence. Calvinists say that in some instances God works directly or indirectly in such a way as to insure that a particular decision will be made. Arminians disagree.

Read the following verses, asking yourself which of the two views appears correct.

*And the Lord said to Moses, "When you go back to Egypt see that you perform before Pharaoh all the wonders which I have put in your power; but I will harden his heart so that he will not let the people go." (Exod. 4:21)*

*And the Lord had given the people favor in the sight of the Egyptians, so that they let them have their request. Thus they plundered the Egyptians. (Exod. 12:36)*

*He turned their heart to hate His people, to deal craftily with His servants. (Ps. 105:25)*

*The king's heart is like channels of water in the hand of the Lord; He turns it wherever He wishes. (Prov. 21:1)*

*The Most High is ruler over the realm of mankind, and bestows it on whomever He wishes. (Dan. 4:25)*

*If a trumpet is blown in a city will not the people tremble? If a calamity occurs in a city has not the Lord done it? (Amos 3:6)*

*For truly in this city there were gathered together against Thy holy servant Jesus, whom Thou didst anoint, both Herod and Pontius Pilate, along with the Gentiles and the people of Israel, to do whatever Thy hand and Thy purpose predestined to occur. (Acts 4:27-28)*

Now let us face the more difficult question as to whether God makes the choice as to who will be saved. Once again, I quote the verses without comment.

*But as Many as received Him, to them He gave the right to become children of God... who were born not of blood, nor of the will of the flesh, nor of the will of man, but of God. (John 1:13)*

*For just as the Father raises the dead and gives them life, even so the Son also gives life to whom He wishes. (John 5:21)*

*For this cause they could not believe, for Isaiah said again, "He has blinded their eyes, and He hardened their heart; lest they see with their eyes, and perceive with their heart, and be converted, and I heal them. (John 12:39-40)*

*And when the Gentiles heard this, they began rejoicing and glorifying the word of the Lord; and as many as had been appointed to eternal life believed. (Acts 13:48)*

*What if God, although willing to demonstrate His wrath and to make His power known, endured with much patience vessels of wrath prepared for destruction? And He did so in order that He might make known the riches of His glory upon vessels of mercy, which He prepared beforehand for glory, even us whom He also called, not from among Jews only, but also among Gentiles. (Rom. 9:22-24)*

*Just as He chose us in Him before the foundation of the world, that we should be holy and blameless before Him. (Eph. 1:4)*

*But we should always give thanks to God for you, brethren beloved by the Lord, because God has chosen you from the beginning for salvation through sanctification by the Spirit and faith in the truth. (2 Thess. 2:13)*

Arminians, needless to say, are well aware of these passages of Scripture and doubtless have explanations for them. What is important to understand is that Calvinism and Arminianism are two systems of theology that cannot be harmonized. Either God made the choice as to who will be saved and then grants man the ability to believe, or the choice is made by man. Either the elect are being saved, or God is saving as many as he can but failing in his purposes. Either God has ordained whatever comes to pass, or, because of man's free will, the best he can do now is adjust himself to evil as it occurs.

## God or the Devil?

What about Wesley's charge that Calvinism makes God to be the devil? Whitefield replied to Wesley in a lengthy letter in which he defended the doctrine of election and particular atonement. Those who are interested in the debate between these two men would profit by reading the full text of both letters. Since Whitefield does not specifically speak to the question of how the work of Satan and the work of God should be distinguished, I shall explain how a Calvinist might do so.

Satan, regardless of how evil his actions, always serves the purposes of God. God frequently uses the devil to serve his higher ends. When Satan taunted God about Job, the Lord allowed Satan to inspire evil men to kill Job's servants and steal his cattle; he gave Satan the power to use wind and lightning to kill Job's children.

In the Books of Daniel and Revelation, when the future actions of the Antichrist and his cohorts (who are controlled by Satan) are predicted, it always says, "It was given to him power." Obviously, Satan serves God's purposes.

Wesley's point, of course, is that Satan desires to have people suffer in hell, and if God decrees the damnation of the ungodly, both God and Satan appear to be working toward the same end. Even here, however, Satan serves God's purposes. If God wills the damnation of the ungodly, he may use Satan in whatever capacity he chooses to fulfill his purposes.

Even Arminians must admit that God allows the devil to have the satisfaction of working toward the damnation of many. Thus, according to Wesley, God stands by unable to prevent Satan from having the satisfaction of seeing multitudes perish. The difference is that the Calvinist believes it is so because God ordained it; the Arminian says it is so because God cannot help it because he has chosen to not interfere directly in the free choices of his creatures.

The devil is also a being filled with only hatred and deceit. He is a rebellious liar and malicious sadist. He desires to see humans suffer for suffering's sake. Thus he always stands in opposition to God even when he does what God ordains.

In contrast, God does not delight in the death of the wicked. He desires that all men be saved and come to the knowledge of the truth.

However, he has chosen to forego the desire to bring all to salvation and has chosen rather to elect only a remnant to eternal life. Why? More important to God than the happiness of man is the desire to display his attributes. He raised Pharaoh up and then hardened the king's heart, "in order to show you My power, and in order to proclaim My name through all the earth" (Exod. 9:16).

Whitefield wrote in his letter, "God taketh no pleasure in the death of sinners, so as to delight simply in their death; but he delights to magnify his justice, by inflicting the punishment which their iniquities have deserved; a righteous judge, who takes not pleasure in condemning a criminal, may yet justly command him to be executed, that the law and justice might be satisfied, even though it may be in his power to procure him a reprieve."[10]

God's other attributes such as mercy, love, and righteousness cannot be fully displayed except against the backdrop of evil. With the entire human race fallen into disobedience and sin, God, though he owed salvation to no one, elected some to eternal life, thereby showing his love and mercy. Then he ordained that Christ publicly die on the cross, "to demonstrate His righteousness" (Rom. 3:25). There every righteous demand that God required for sinners was fully met.

Thus, Paul said that God can now save the wicked and be both "just and the justifier of the one who has faith in Jesus" (Rom. 3:26).

Against the background of the universal sinfulness of the human race, God has not only chosen some to be saved but elevated them to become heirs of God and joint-heirs with Christ. This magnifies God's incredible generosity and meticulous justice. Thus God chose to do what he did, "in order that the manifold wisdom of God might now be made known through the church to the rulers and authorities in the heavenly places. This was in accordance with the eternal purpose which He carried out in Christ Jesus our Lord" (Eph. 3:10-11).

Though we can see that believers will display the manifold wisdom of God, it is not clear to us how unbelievers will do so. We are told only that the wrath of man will praise God, and in Proverbs we read, "The Lord has made everything for its own purpose, even the wicked for the day of evil" (16:4).

If we ask why God elected so few to eternal life in contrast to the great masses of humanity, we cannot answer. Luther, you will recall, said that the greatest degree of faith is exercised when we believe that God is merciful even though he saves so few and damns so many.

Thankfully, no one reading these words need wonder if he or she is among the "elect." When we come to Christ with humility and faith, He has promised to receive us. In coming to Him we give evidence that the Holy Spirit is at work in our hearts. All who desire to be saved can be:

"But as many as received Him, to them He gave the right to become children of God, even to those who believe in His name, who were born not of blood, nor of the will of the flesh, nor of the will of man, but of God" (John 1:12-13).

*Oh, the depth of the riches both of wisdom and knowledge of God! How unsearchable are His judgments and unfathomable His ways! For who has known the mind of the Lord, or who became His counselor? Or who has first given to Him that it might be paid back to Him again? For from Him and through Him and to Him are all things. To Him be glory forever. Amen. (Rom. 11:33-36)*

Let us take Luther's advice and stand in awe of God.

### Notes

1. Arnold A. Dallimore, *George Whitefield* (Westchester, Ill.: Crossway Books, 1980), 2:5-41.
2. Ibid., 1:309-312.
3. William G. McLoughlin, "Introduction" in *Charles Finney's Lectures on Revivals of Religion* (Cambridge: Belknap Press, 1960), xii.
4. Dallimore, 2:511-512.
5. "Clark Pinnock's Response" in *Predestination and Free Will,* eds. David Basinger and Randall Basinger (Downers Grove, Ill.: InterVarsity Press, 1986), 58.
6. Norman L. Geisler, "God, Evil and Dispensations" in *Walvoord: A Tribute,* ed. Donald Campbell (Chicago: Moody Press, 1980), 102-103.
7. Pinnock, 149.
8. D. A. Carson, *Divine Sovereignty and Human Responsibility* (Atlanta: John Knox Press, 1981), 184.
9. Pinnock, 150.
10. Dallimore, 2:567.

# THIRTEEN

# Can a Saved Person Ever Be Lost?

So you are saved, a born-again Christian with the assurance that Christ is your Savior. Can you ever be lost? Can the decision you made be reversed either because you choose to turn away from Christ or because you fall into apostasy or moral failure? Some Christians cherish a belief in what is called "eternal security," while others call it a "hellish doctrine" that lulls Christians into spiritual lethargy and carnality. After all, they reason, if a person knows he is assured a place in heaven, he will be tempted to neglect the disciplines of holiness and opt to live carelessly in the world. One preacher even said that eternal security should not be publicly taught even if it is true; better to keep Christians alert by warning them about falling away than to tell them they have a room reserved in heaven that can never be canceled regardless of their life-style.

Whether or not you believe in eternal security depends on where you stand on the free-will controversy. Those who say that salvation depends on our choice alone, usually quite logically conclude that we can lose our salvation. The free will that accepts Christ is the same free will that can reject him. It is my choice to be saved and it is my choice to be "unsaved" too.

Arminianism is the name most often associated with the belief that a saved person can eventually be lost. Yet Arminius himself did not teach this doctrine explicitly. He simply said that it was an open question. He thought that Calvinists who believed that all the saints would persevere had no right to be so certain.

John Wesley, who was greatly influenced by Arminius and stressed freedom of the will, was more definite. He strongly believed that a saved person could be lost in everlasting perdition.

Daniel Whedon, an American theologian and recognized spokesman for Methodism, wrote: "In full consistency with that doctrine of human freedom and responsibility which pervades our theology, we maintain that, inasmuch as we were free in first performing the conditions of salvation, so we are free in the continuance or cessation of their performance."[1] He said that time and again we shall be tested as to whether or not we will hold fast our initial commitment. Some will and some won't.

Methodists, following Wesley, believe that God does give sufficient grace to persevere, but that it is up to us as to whether or not we receive this grace. We can, at any time, choose against God and be lost.

But at what point does a person cross the line and lose his salvation? Among the many groups that teach this doctrine, there are at least three answers given. The first says I am saved until I sin again; then I lose my salvation. I sat next to a man on a plane who was taught this as a child. He went to bed fearful that he had committed some sin that he had not confessed. If he died during the night he would be damned. When he reached his teens, he realized that he could never hope to "stay saved," so he decided to leave the faith until some future date, possibly just before he died. "I'm on furlough from living the Christian life," he told me.

Dr. Harry Ironside, for many years the pastor of Moody Church in Chicago, said he met a man who claimed he had been saved ninety-nine times! Actually, if you believe you lose your salvation every time you sin, I'm surprised it wasn't more like 999 (perhaps with a zero added)! We can sympathize with that pastor who told the drunk who got saved every Sunday, "Next week I ought to shoot you right after you get saved, so that you'd be sure of heaven!"

Fortunately, most of those who believe in conditional security (namely that a believer can lose his salvation if he doesn't persevere in holiness) do not take it that far. If we lost our salvation each time we sinned, the gospel would not be good news but a message of uncertainty and fear. Assurance of salvation would forever elude us.

Most Arminians take a second, more moderate position. They say that a person loses his salvation when he commits willful sin. Such a sin can only be committed when one is (1) knowingly disobedient and (2) refuses to confess the sin and thereby continues in disobedience. Some also add another condition: (3) it must be an act, not merely a sinful thought. Presumably, then, one could sin willfully without placing his salvation in jeopardy if the sin was immediately confessed, or if it were just a sin of the mind.

Third, there are those who believe that only those who fall into serious apostasy will be lost. Other sins do not separate us from Christ, but willfully denying him—deliberately spurning the blood of Christ—is the point at which salvation is forfeited.

One difficulty shared by all of the above views is that the line of demarcation is unclear. What is the difference between a willful sin and one that is not willful? What constitutes denying Christ? And, does one know when he or she has crossed the line?

## Conditional Security

Ask the average churchgoer whether a saved person can be lost and the discussion will usually center around several puzzling passages of Scripture. Perhaps the most controversial and best known is Hebrews 6:1-6. The author wrote that in the case of those who have begun in the Christian life "and then have fallen away, it is impossible to renew them again to repentance, since they again crucify to themselves the Son of God, and put Him to open shame" (v. 6). Arminians use this text to prove that believers can fall away and be lost forever. Some go on to teach that such a person cannot be saved a second time because of the words "it is impossible to renew them again to repentance." However, there is a better way to explain this phrase as will be seen in a moment.

Some Calvinists, in order to preserve the doctrine of eternal security, have taught that the people spoken of were not Christians in the first place. Those who have "fallen away" are ones who benefited from the Christian faith but did not personally embrace it. Though many fine scholars hold to such an interpretation, an impartial reading of the text leads to the conclusion that the preceding description applies to believers. Yes, believers can fall away. But the question is, what did the writer mean by "fall away"? Did he mean to fall away into hell? The context makes it clear that this is not what the writer had in mind. He used the same expression for the Israelites who fell away in the desert (3:12). Their "falling away " did not determine their eternal destiny but resulted in earthly chastisement and loss of blessing.

The Book of Hebrews was written to those who were tempted to revert back to the Old Testament sacrificial system. They were beginning to doubt whether Christ was fully sufficient; whether he did in fact replace the rituals and sacrifices required by the law. To have such doubts indicated unbelief and hardness of heart. To return to the Old Testament rituals and sacrificial system was to "again crucify to themselves the Son of God, and put Him to open shame."

The writer went on to explain that they could not fall

back on Old Testament sacrifices and simultaneously be brought to repentance. That is, they could not be restored to fellowship with God *while* they were offering lambs on the altar (crucifying Christ afresh). But if they ceased these practices, there is no reason to suggest that they could not be restored. Yes, believers can fall away, but not to eternal damnation.

An equally controversial passage is in Hebrews 10:26-31, where those who go on sinning after they have received the knowledge of the truth are told that they can expect terrifying judgment. Under the law of Moses people died if they broke the law. In contrast, "How much severer punishment do you think he will deserve who has trampled under foot the Son of God, and has regarded as unclean the blood of the covenant by which he was sanctified, and has insulted the Spirit of grace?" (v. 29).

There are two reasons why we must interpret this passage to refer to believers. First, the author said, "If *we* go on sinning," which implies willful rebellion was also a possibility for him. Second, this disobedient person has been sanctified by the blood of the covenant. Here is a believer sinning against so much greater light, thus the punishment must be more severe. But what could constitute "severer punishment"? This passage shows the extent to which God is willing to discipline his own people. There are forms of divine retribution that are worse than physical death—there is anguish of soul— mental and spiritual torment—that makes death a welcome relief.

The physical discipline of the Old Testament did not necessarily determine one's eternal destiny. We should not think that all Israelites except Moses, Joshua, and Caleb ended in eternal perdition. God frequently disciplined his own people with severe punishment. Since the New Covenant is so much greater than the Old, those who believe and then turn away deserve greater chastisement. Though all believers are shielded from God's eternal wrath because of Christ, they are not exempt from severe discipline, including death. As there was physical and mental discipline under the Old Covenant, so there is even greater discipline in the New. Both are temporal, not eternal.

Of course, there are other texts that Arminians use to prove that the eventual salvation of a believer is dependent on whether or not he continues to pursue godliness. Christ says, regarding those branches that cease to abide in him, that men "gather them and cast them into the fire, and they are burned" (John 15:6). Here are branches who were "in Christ" but now find themselves severed from him and burned.

Calvinists usually make one of two replies. These branches may represent people who have only a superficial relationship with Christ but who truly never were saved. Often branches appear to be authentic but are actually parasites that are not part of the vine's root system. Another possibility is that these are true believers, but the fire referred to is not the fire of hell but the fire that will eventually try believers at the judgment seat of Christ. At any rate, it is somewhat presumptuous to build a case for or against eternal security on a metaphor lest we press the analogy beyond what the Lord intended.

Perhaps the most scholarly defense of conditional security is the book *Life in the Son* by Robert Shank.[2] The book turns on two premises: (1) only those who continue in obedience and faith will be saved, and (2) some believers fall away and therefore will eventually be lost. The author stresses the dozens of verses in the New Testament that link salvation with an ongoing commitment. For example, Christ said, "Truly, truly, I say to you, if anyone keeps my word he shall never see death" (John 8:51). Or consider the words of Paul, who after telling his readers that they were reconciled to God, added, "if indeed you continue in the faith firmly established and steadfast, and not moved away from the hope of the gospel that you have heard" (Col. 1:23). Here, and in countless other places, eternal life appears to be conditioned upon a life of obedience.

Think this through carefully: historic Calvinism agrees with Shank that continual obedience is necessary for salvation. It affirms that all true believers do in fact continue in such obedience. Other Calvinists disagree and teach that true believers can indeed backslide and even turn away from Christ. The conditional passages are interpreted to refer to a loss of blessing and rewards. Obedience is necessary for rewards and is essential if one is to follow though with becoming a disciple of Christ. Abiding, obeying, keeping—these are necessary for growth and blessing, but unfortunately some believers are carnal and do not go on to spiritual obedience. These experience the discipline of God, and if they do not change their ways they will lose their reward and be saved "so as by fire." Though all believers have some fruit in their lives, some have very little. Yet they too will be saved. These scholars stress "eternal security"; a true believer is saved no matter what. The interpretation of the passages in Hebrews given a few pages back essentially agrees with this second shade of Calvinism.

To put it differently, though all Calvinists believe that the truly saved will never be lost, there is disagreement over the question of the extent to which a believer can backslide. Historic Calvinism stresses the "perseverance of the saints," namely that true believers never fall away, and if they do, it is not for long. If a person fails to continue in the faith, he is giving proof that he was never saved. As mentioned, these Calvinists agree with Shank that obedience is a condition for salvation, but then they go on to assert that the truly saved person does, in fact, live a life of obedience. Some go so far as to say that there are no carnal Christians.

This involves us with the same difficulties as the Arminians in trying to distinguish between minor sins and major ones. The Arminian does this to determine the point at which a person loses his or her salvation. Some Calvinists do it to determine whose faith is spurious and whose is genuine. Unfortunately, some Calvinists have been so insistent that the proof of regeneration is pursuing holiness that they seem to make good works a part of salvation. Charles Hodge went so far as to say, "There is a perpetual danger of falling. . . . Neither members of the church nor the elect can be saved unless they persevere in holiness, and they cannot persevere in holiness without continual watchfulness and effort."[3] Ironically, though Hodge was a strong Calvinist, this statement could be applauded by any Arminian! By stressing the need for good works, some Calvinists seem to agree with the Arminians that Christ's work on the cross made only a down payment for our salvation and we must keep up the installments.

As mentioned, other Calvinists prefer the term "eternal security," which stresses that those who are truly regenerated will be eternally saved, even if they fail to persevere in holiness, and fall into carnality and failure. This view sees good works as confirming evidence of regeneration but in no way contributing to the free gift of salvation given to those who believe. Those who say they have believed but exhibit no fruit of the Spirit and no appetite for prayer and God's Word have ample reason to doubt whether they were truly saved, but then again they might be true believers. Christians have been known to fall into doctrinal and moral failure. Some have rebelled against God and have been taken away in death (1 Cor. 11:30).

The purpose of this chapter is to underscore the differences between Calvinism and Arminianism; thus we leave our discussion of this disagreement. Those interested in these two viewpoints should consult resource materials listed at the end of this book. The point to be made is that both kinds of Calvinists agree on the central issue: all true believers will be saved. Arminians disagree.

Are there passages that explicitly teach that all true believers will be saved? We have briefly considered passages used by Arminians, so now we will consider some that are often quoted by Calvinists.

## Unconditional Security

Unconditional security teaches that the God who chose his people unto eternal life will indeed lose none; they who have been redeemed by the blood of Christ will assuredly be saved.

Though this belief is most often associated with Calvin, it was held by Whitefield, Edwards, and a host of others who believed that one of God's elect could never be lost. It was, you will recall, the last of the five points of Calvinism affirmed by the Synod of Dort. There it was spoken of as perseverance of the saints, the belief that all who truly believe will persevere in grace until the end. A number of passages have been used to prove this doctrine.

First, there are the direct statements of Christ.

*My sheep hear My voice, and I know them, and they follow Me; and I give eternal life to them, and they shall never perish; and no one shall snatch them out of My hand. My Father, who has given them to Me, is greater than all; and no one is able to snatch them out of the Father's hand. (John 10:27-29)*

The Father and the Son are well able to protect the sheep since they are greater than the enemies who would destroy them.

Arminians say that while no enemy can take us from God's hand, we are able to remove ourselves from the Father's hand by our disobedience. We came to Christ of our own free will; we can leave the same way.

Calvinists say that the gift of salvation is irrevocable. We cannot slip through one of God's fingers because *we are*

*one of his fingers!* We have been inseparably joined to
Christ, members of his body, of his flesh, and of his bones.
Even if, in a moment of depression, a believer wished to
be removed from Christ, God is not obligated to grant him
his wish. Since God made the choice as to who will be
saved, he also has the right to preserve the elect regardless
of their rebellion.

To put it differently, what would you think of a shepherd
who was given one hundred sheep in the morning and
returned in the evening with ninety-two? He would be
ridiculed for his carelessness, weakness, and failure to
carry out his basic responsibilities. Often sheep do go
astray; others follow false paths made by robbers who
seek to lure them from the flock. But a competent
shepherd knows all that. He keeps a watchful eye on each
sheep, and when it strays he brings it back by hook or by
crook!

Do we think that the Good Shepherd is unable to keep
the sheep entrusted to him? It is unthinkable that some of
these sheep that are a gift from the Father to the Son will
not be in the fold at nightfall. As Christ said elsewhere,
"And this is the will of Him who sent Me, that of all that He
has given Me I lose nothing, but raise it up on the last day"
(John 6:39).

It is reasonable to assume that God granted all the
requests of Christ. If so, let us remember that he explicitly
prayed that none of those whom God had given him be
lost (John 17:11-12). And lest we think that the human
will is so strong that it can thwart the purposes of God,
Christ, in speaking of himself to the Father, affirmed,
"Glorify Thy Son . . . even as Thou gavest Him authority
over all mankind, that to all whom Thou hast given Him,
He may give eternal life" (John 17:1-2). His authority
extends to every individual. Therefore he has the power
to give eternal life to the elect.

In Romans chapter 8, Paul used five words to describe
God's work on behalf of his people. "For whom He fore-

knew, He also predestined to become conformed to the
image of His Son, that He might be the first-born among
many brethren; and whom He predestinated, these He
also called; and whom He called, these He also justified;
and whom He justified, these He also glorified" (vv.
29-30). The five words are: (1) *Foreknew.* We have
learned that this means more than the fact that God
knows the future; it is used only of people, never for God's
knowledge of events or things. It means that there are
those whom God "fore-loved." (2) We were *predestined.*
These he predestined, or marked out beforehand, to be
conformed to the image of his Son. The next word, (3)
*called,* refers to God's effectual call to salvation. This
word stands in the middle of the five because the "call" is
the means by which God brings the salvation to the hearts
of individuals. The first two words speak about God's
plans in eternity past; the call makes it actual and the
result is (4) *justification,* that is, those who are called are
now declared righteous. And those who are justified, God
has already (5) *glorified.*

Stifler says that these words provide "five golden links
connecting God's gracious purpose in eternity past with
its consummation in the eternity to come."[4] Each link
takes the elect to a further stage until the end. Those
whom he began with are the same as those with whom he
ended. No one falls between the cracks. Those whom he
foreknew are the ones he glorified.

Notice the certainty of God's purpose: the word
*glorified* is in the past tense. As far as God is concerned
the saints are already in heaven, for God "calls into being
that which does not exist" (Rom. 4:17). Paul said elsewhere that we are in Christ and seated with him in the
heavenly places in Christ Jesus (Eph. 2:6). The only way
the saints can be thrown out of heaven is if Christ himself
were banned because they are already in him, members of
his body, and seated with him at the throne.

Of course, there are other proofs for the security of the

believer. The Holy Spirit is both a pledge of our inheritance (Eph. 1:14) as well as a seal unto the day of redemption (Eph. 4:30). The former means that we are given a down payment with the guarantee that there is more to come. We have been given a drop as proof that we shall someday have the ocean. The seal of the Spirit means that the arrival of believers in heaven is guaranteed. Though Satan, the world, the flesh, and the devil may try to tamper with the seal, believers shall arrive at their intended destination.

There is no legal loophole by which God can get out of his obligations to those whom he has chosen to save. He cannot cast off those whom he has elected to eternal life. Having begun a work in his people, he will complete it. The unfaithfulness of man cannot frustrate the eternal purposes of God (Phil. 1:6).

Arthur Pink put it this way, "For any of the elect to perish would necessarily entail a *defeated Father,* who was balked of the realization of his purpose; a *disappointed Son,* who would never see the full travail of his soul and be satisfied; and a *disgraced Spirit,* who had failed to preserve those entrusted to his care. From such awful errors may we be delivered."[5] So may it be.


## The Doctrine of Assurance

To believe that the elect will be saved is one thing; to know that one is indeed a member of that company is another.

Can one know that he or she has savingly believed? John, in his epistle, taught this was indeed possible. "These things I have written to you who believe in the name of the Son of God, in order that you may know that you have eternal life" (1 John 5:13). Surely God, who has given us a detailed revelation would not leave us in doubt about the most important question we could possibly ponder. We are talking about damnation or glory, hell or heaven.

The Roman Catholic church strongly rejects the doctrine of eternal security. Augustine wrote about the gift of perseverance, yet also denied that one can have assurance of his final salvation. At the Council of Trent in 1546, the church said that God does not forsake the one who has been once justified "unless he be first forsaken by them." An example is a mortal sin which causes a sinner to forfeit salvation, although he may be *re*justified if he meets certain requirements.

There is an obvious connection between eternal security and assurance. Since Catholics agree that even the most devout can commit a mortal sin, there can be no settled assurance that one will in fact be in heaven. Those who believe they have assurance have been accused by Rome of the sin of presumption.

The matter of eternal security of the elect has already been discussed, but still the question is, How do I know that I am among the secure? How can I know?

There are three witnesses that will help us know where we stand. The first is the promises of Christ, who said that those who believe on him would have eternal life. To *believe* means "to rely upon" or "to trust."

Two clarifications are in order. First, there must be an acknowledgment of personal need; an understanding of one's sinfulness and helplessness without Christ. His work on the cross was a substitutionary sacrifice for sinners. Without it, no one can be saved. But only those who see their need qualify. Christ came not to call the righteous but sinners to repentance. Second, faith must be directed to Christ alone. Some who claim to trust Christ also have confidence in baptism, in the Mass, in good works. The amount of faith is not as important as the object of faith.

Let it also be said that this faith is not a prayer (though it may be expressed through prayer). Many who have

prayed to "receive Christ" are unconverted simply because
they think saying the right words saves them. All the
prayers that have ever been said by all the people in the
world have not changed God's mind about a single sinner.
It is the transfer of trust that saves.

The second witness is the Holy Spirit. "The Spirit Himself bears witness with our spirit that we are the children
of God" (Rom. 8:16). The Holy Spirit not only regenerates
but also comes to indwell every believer. The new nature
received at conversion is thus energized by the indwelling
Spirit. This begins the process of spiritual growth. A
personal sense of the Spirit's presence, whether dramatic
or quietly peaceful, usually accompanies the gift of salvation. An inner certainty comes within the human heart.

Finally, there is the fruit of the new life—the works that
accompany salvation. These are not uniform in the lives of
the converted. Some experience dramatic growth through
proper teaching and a strong desire for Christian fellowship and a personal knowledge of God. Others may wan-
der in a spiritual wilderness, without any guidance in
their newfound faith. Still others may fall back into old
habits and sinful attitudes. But almost always there is
some outer change brought about by the new life within.
If there is no change whatever, the person should examine
himself to see whether he has indeed savingly believed.

To say that the doctrines of eternal security and assurance lead to worldliness (because people will want to get
their ticket to heaven and yet live for all the pleasures of
earth before they get there) is to misunderstand profoundly the radical change conversion produces. The
Spirit changes the sinner's disposition and desires, so that
the pleasures of the world lose their attraction. And even
when the grace of God is misused, as it sometimes is, the
true believer will live in misery. The lower nature continues to desire sin; but the new nature desires righteousness.

Furthermore, God disciplines those who live in willful

sin through the inevitable consequences of sin and through those troublesome experiences of life that drive his children back into fellowship. The Judgment Seat of Christ, at which all believers will appear some day, will test all works and attitudes by fire. This for some will be a time of deep regret and even shame. God does not take lightly the responsibility believers have to live up to their calling.

May God help us to "make our calling and election sure" by our submission to Christ and his Word.

## Notes

1. Daniel D. Whedon, "Doctrines of Methodism," in *Wesleyan Theology*, ed. Thomas a Longford (Durham, N.C.: The Labyrinth Press, 1984), 100.
2. Robert Shank, *Life in the Son* (Springfield, Mo.: Westcott Publishers, 1960).
3. Quoted in Arthur W. Pink, *Eternal Security* (Grand Rapids: Baker, 1974), 84.
4. James A. Stifler, *The Epistle to the Romans* (Chicago: Moody Press, 1960), 149.
5. Pink, 17.

# CONCLUSION

These chapters are an attempt to clarify some of the doctrinal differences that date back to the early centuries of the Christian church. There are other present-day disagreements, such as the inerrancy of Scripture, the role of women in the church, the validity of the gift of tongues, to name a few. But those discussed in this book represent some of the earliest and most important controversies, and they still divide Christendom.

Today tolerance is regarded much more highly than doctrinal accuracy. We have grown accustomed to Christian talk shows that are rich in experience but devoid of serious doctrinal content. Indeed, one of the cardinal rules of the Christian media is that all doctrinal content, if there is any, must be reduced to the lowest common denominator. Even when the masses are told to believe in Christ, they know very little about the whys and wherefores.

It is perhaps for this reason that we see such a marked decline in commitment on the part of those who "make a profession of Christ." We have substituted a popular easy-believism for sound doctrinal teaching. People are believing in Christ but have little understanding of what

salvation is all about. They become easy prey for the many
false cults and doctrinal misrepresentations popular today.

As I write, the New Age movement is making significant
inroads into Christianity. It is popular to believe that one
can adopt some of the religious presuppositions of eastern
religions and still be a good Christian. The uniqueness of
Christianity is almost wholly lost in the mindless quest for
religious experience, regardless of the source.

If students of prophecy are correct, a false worldwide
religion will eventually dominate the world. All that needs
to happen is for Christians, or at least those who affirm
the title, to simply fall prey to the notion that the real
curse in the church is not doctrinal error but division.
Consumed with a desire for unity, doctrinal matters will
be pushed aside. Experience will be the one factor that
will unify all Christians and eventually bring all religions
of the world under one umbrella.

This might explain why serious doctrinal thinking has
already become subordinate to the experience-centered
narcissism of our times. We are raising a generation of
Christians that sees no contradiction in affirming faith in
Christ on Sunday and feeding their craving for sensuality
during the week. Witness the moral scandals of some of
our religious leaders and you must agree that much of our
Christianity is a mile wide and an inch deep.

What can we do to halt this decline? How can we teach
our young people so that they will not be mesmerized by
the vision of unity but insist on doctrinal and moral
integrity?

First, we must teach them the distinctives of Christianity
from the Bible and give them an appreciation for those
who have preceded them in the history of the church. We
must disprove the old adage that says that the only thing
we can learn from history is that we do not learn from
history. Of course we can learn from history; we are
derelict if we don't. The battles of the past give us some
appreciation for how we can face the enemy in the future.

We must be both instructed and motivated by those who stood firm in the midst of pressures not unlike ours today.

Second, we must return to a simple rule of logic: a thing cannot both be and not be in the same way and at the same time. It is contradictory to say that Christ can both be the only way to God and yet there are other ways, too. It is absurd to claim that Christianity can somehow be amalgamated with reincarnationalism, moral relativism, or astrology.

Finally, we must provide authentic models of Christian living. We ourselves must demonstrate the integration of Christian doctrine and life-style. When the Pharisees doubted Christ's teachings, he challenged them to observe the consistency between what he taught and the works he did. Indeed, if they just believed the works alone, they would have had to conclude that his doctrine was correct. "If I do not do the works of My Father, do not believe Me; but if I do them, though you do not believe Me, believe the works; that you may know and understand that the Father is in Me, and I in the Father" (John 10:37-38).

Doubtless, many who read this book will disagree with my conclusions. But if what I have written will in some small way contribute to theological discussion, my efforts will have been well rewarded.

My plea is that theology be restored as the queen of the sciences. That is another way of saying that we should never tire of discussing ultimate issues. Our eternal fate and the destiny of the world hinges on a correct understanding of the matters discussed in this book.

Let us strive for a clear understanding of what the Bible teaches. Only then can we be successful in the things that matter most.

# SELECTED BIBLIOGRAPHY

Abbott, S. J., ed. *The Documents of Vatican II.* Translated by Joseph
    Gallagher. New York: The Guild Press, 1966. This book contains the
    message and meaning of the Second Ecumenical Council of the
    Catholic Church. These documents set the tone for the current
    changes taking place within this branch of Christendom.

Basinger, David, and Randall Basinger, eds. *Predestination and Free
    Will.* Downers Grove, Ill.: InterVarsity Press, 1986. A debate between
    four scholars, each presenting a different perspective on the topic
    of predestination and free will. The differences between Calvinism
    and Arminianism are clarified, and the practical applications of each
    doctrine are described. Essays are written by John Feinberg,
    Norman Geisler, Bruce Reichenbach, and Clark Pinnock.

Bennett, C. P. *The New Saint Joseph Baltimore Catechism.* New York:
    Catholic Book Publishing Co., 1962. A clear summary of basic
    Catholic dogma as taught prior to Vatican II. Excellent for reference
    and clarification of Rome's teaching.

Berkhof, Louis. *The History of Christian Doctrines.* Grand Rapids:
    Baker, 1937. Summarizes the history of Christian doctrine topically.
    Excellent introductory textbook.

Berkouwer, G. C. *Divine Election.* Grand Rapids: Eerdmans, 1960. A
    scholarly but highly readable defense of the reformed doctrine of
    predestination. Answers objections often leveled at Calvinism.

Boettner, Lorraine. *Roman Catholicism.* Phillipsburg, N.J.: Presbyterian
    and Reformed Publishing Co., 1962. An evaluation of the doctrines
    of Rome in light of history and the New Testament. Does not take
    into account more recent changes within the Catholic church.

Bromiley, Geoffrey. *Children of Promise.* Grand Rapids: Eerdmans,
    1979. Possibly the best defense of infant baptism available. Argues
    that infant baptism in the New Testament, like circumcision in the
    Old, is a sign of the Covenant.

Jewett, Paul K. *Infant Baptism and the Covenant of Grace.* Grand Rapids: Eerdmans, 1977. This contains a detailed history of the doctrine of infant baptism and concludes that it is contrary to the teachings of the New Testament. This book is of first-rate scholarship. It is interesting in that it comes from the pen of a covenant theologian, who was trained to accept infant baptism. This is necessary reading for anyone who has an interest in this controversial doctrine.

Langford, Thomas, ed. *Wesleyan Theology: A Source Book.* Durham, N.C., The Labyrinth Press, 1984. A series of essays by various scholars on Wesleyan theology. Helpful as a contemporary analysis of the great preacher's theology.

Luther, Martin. *The Bondage of the Will.* Grand Rapids: Baker, 1976. This is one of Luther's best works. He assailed Erasmus for defending free will and asserts that salvation is wholly of God. He argued that those who believe in free will do not understand the gospel.

Ott, Ludwig. *Fundamentals of Catholic Dogma.* Translated by Patrick Lynch. St. Louis: B. Herder Book Co., 1957. A textbook of Catholic theology. Gives a careful discussion of each doctrine along with its rationale. Contains many quotations from the church fathers and is well outlined.

Owen, John. *The Death of Death in the Death of Christ.* 1648. Reprint. London: The Banner of Truth Trust, 1952. Introduction by J. I. Packer. This book is the fruit of seven years of intensive study and concludes that Christ died only for the elect. Indeed, Owen held that any other view was destructive to the gospel. Though difficult reading, we cannot teach that an atonement was made for all men until we wrestle with Owen's biblical and logical arguments. The introduction by J. I. Packer is worth the price of this volume.

Pink, Arthur. *Eternal Security.* Grand Rapids: Baker, 1974. A defense of the Reformed doctrine of the perseverance of the saints. Argues that all true believers persevere, and therefore so-called carnal believers and those who turn from the faith were never truly converted.

Piper, John. *The Justification of God.* Grand Rapids: Baker, 1983. A scholarly and thorough treatment of Paul's defense of God's righteousness in Romans 9:1-23. The author shows why all Arminian attempts to interpret this passage fail to do justice to the text.

Shank, Robert. *Life in the Son.* Springfield, Mo.: Westcott, 1960. An interesting theological defense of conditional security. Argues that only believers who persevere will be saved. Others, who fall away, though at one time genuinely converted, will be eternally lost.

Shelley, Bruce. *Church History in Plain Language.* Waco, Tex.: Word Books, 1982. A readable history of Christianity that emphasizes both the prominent people and events that have shaped the church throughout the centuries.

Sproul, R. C. *Chosen by God.* Wheaton, Ill.: Tyndale House, 1986. This is a highly readable study on the doctrine of predestination. Defends and clarifies Calvinism.

Verduin, Leonard. *The Reformers and Their Stepchildren.* Grand
Rapids: Eerdmans, 1964. A fascinating account of the Anabaptist
movement before and during the Reformation. Explains the role of
theology in keeping the church and state united. The author teaches
that the reformers did not go far enough in ridding the church from
medieval influences. This book should be read by every Christian
interested in the purity of the church.
Warfield, Benjamin. *The Plan of Salvation.* Grand Rapids: Eerdmans,
10th printing, 1977. A classic study of the basic and essential
differences between various theories of salvation such as sacramentalism, Calvinism, and Pelagianism. Should be read by everyone who
cares to understand the most essential doctrine of the Bible.

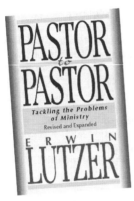

# PASTOR TO PASTOR
*Tackling the Problems of Ministry*
*Revised and Expanded*

The role of the pastor as both leader and teacher is often complicated by many difficult situations and problematic issues. Well-known pastor and conference speaker Erwin Lutzer offers practical advice on how to handle issues such as:

- church splits
- burnout
- worship styles
- congregational expectations

- pastoral priorities
- politics
- church boards
- counseling

This revised edition provides encouragement and solutions to help pastors better serve God and their churches. In working through difficult situations of ministry, pastors and congregations can both grow spiritually.

"Don't speed read this book. Pause, ponder, pray—and grow!"
                                            —Warren W. Wiersbe

Available at your local Christian bookstore or

PUBLICATIONS

P.O. Box 2607 • Grand Rapids, MI 49501